MW01274444

National Welfare and National Decay

NATIONAL WELFARE AND NATIONAL DECAY

NATIONAL WELFARE
AND
NATIONAL DECAY

WILLIAM McDOUGALL, F.R.S.

PROFESSOR OF PSYCHOLOGY IN HARVARD UNIVERSITY,
FORMERLY READER IN MENTAL PHILOSOPHY
IN THE UNIVERSITY OF OXFORD

METHUEN & CO. LTD.
36 ESSEX STREET W.C.
LONDON

First Published in 1921

FOREWORD TO THE ENGLISH EDITION

THIS little book contains the substance of six lectures given at the Lowell Institute of Boston, in the spring of 1921, and afterwards published under the title " Is America Safe for Democracy ? " In preparing an English Edition at the request of Messrs. Methuen, I have slightly altered a few passages to adapt the book for British readers.

The demographic problem of America is more complicated than that of Britain by reason of the existence of the coloured part of the population and the immense flood of immigration which now for many years has threatened to bring about a complete racial substitution of the American stock. But, apart from these complications, the same fundamental danger threatens both nations, as indeed it threatens, in lesser degree perhaps, all other civilized nations, namely, the danger of the deterioration of the innate qualities of the population.

Many excellent books have been published, urging the claims of " eugenics," since Francis Galton first stirred the conscience of Europe and America on the problem of the preservation of

v

human qualities. Most of these books have been written from the purely biological standpoint. They give excellent accounts of the principles of natural selection, of heredity, and of the Mendelian laws. It has seemed to me that a presentation of the case for eugenics from a more psychological standpoint and on a broad historical background might usefully supplement these biological treatises. For, important as are the facts and principles of physical heredity, the general reader may have some difficulty in connecting the processes of cell-division, the chromosomes of the fruit-fly, or the coat-colours of piebald guinea-pigs, with the spiritual endowment of mankind. I have therefore brought together in these few lectures the findings of mental anthropology, which are now beginning to be garnered on a large scale ; and I have tried to indicate, in as impartial and scientific a manner as is possible in this still obscure field, their bearing upon the great problems of national welfare and national decay. I have added in footnotes some evidential matter which may be neglected by the cursory reader ; and in appendices I have put forward certain proposals which, if they could be put into practice, would, I think, go far to remedy the present disastrous state of affairs. The last of these appendices is a reprint of an article which appear in *Scribner's Magazine* for October, 1921. I am indebted to the editor of that magazine for permission to reproduce the article in these pages.

I would especially draw the attention of readers

FOREWORD

interested in political, economic, or social science
to the evidence cited in this volume, which indicates
very strongly, if it does not finally prove, that the
social stratification which exists in modern industrial communities is positively correlated with a
corresponding stratification of innate moral and
intellectual quality, or, in less technical language,
that the upper social strata, as compared with
the lower, contain a larger proportion of persons
of superior natural endowments. This is a proposition which has been stoutly maintained by most
of the eugenists from Galton onward. But it has
been the greatest weakness of the eugenic propaganda that it is so largely founded upon and as-
sumes the truth of this proposition. For the critics
and scorners of eugenics have vehemently denied
it, or poured ridicule upon it ; and no proof of it
was available for their refutation. In a paper read
before the Eugenics Education Society in London
("Psychology in the Service of Eugenics," *Eugenics Review*, January, 1914) I pointed out that
this great gap in the eugenist argument could only
be filled by applying the methods of experimental
psychology. Two of my pupils (Mr. C. Burt and
Mr. H. B. English) made the first contribution by
such methods toward the filling of the gap ; and
more recently several similar studies with similar
positive results have been made in America. They
are reported in the following pages.

Harvard College,   W. McD.
Sept., 1921.

NATIONAL WELFARE AND NATIONAL DECAY

INTRODUCTION

THE ISLAND OF EUGENIA: THE PHANTASY OF A FOOLISH PHILOSOPHER

ONE of my children, after reading Mr. McKenna's story of the youth who inherited fifty million pounds sterling and who came to a miserable end, asked me: " Dad, what would you do if you had fifty millions ? " The question brought back to my mind a scheme which I had conceived in the enthusiasm of youth and had even committed to paper. That paper had lain forgotten for thirty years. But, stimulated by my child's question, I found it among piles of unpublished manuscript. Having read it through I decided that thirty years' growth of worldly wisdom had not made the scheme, conceived in all the ardour and ignorance of youth, seem any less

The chapter "THE ISLAND OF EUGENIA," which appeared in Messrs. Scribner's Magazine, is published in this book by the courtesy of Messrs. Charles Scribner's Sons.

I

desirable or less practicable. I have therefore recast my original draft, in the form of a dialogue between two men of middle age whom I have named the Philanthropist and the Seer, or the Practical Man and the Scientist.

The Practical Man. My dear old friend, welcome to my summer retreat. I can hardly believe that thirty years have passed since we were room-mates in the old College and discussed so seriously our plans for reforming the world.

The Scientist. No, indeed. It seems but yesterday that we took our great decisions, you to devote yourself to the making of a great fortune, I to give myself wholly to the study of mankind : you with the conviction that science can do little without the power that money gives ; I in the belief that men can easily be led to do the right thing, if only we have certain knowledge to guide them in the choice of what is worth doing.

P. Yes, I remember it all. I did desire the power that money gives ; and in all these years, during which I have been piling up the dollars, I have never forgotten my resolve to make good use of any wealth I might acquire. And now, as you know, I have made my pile, I have been successful. Good fortune, great opportunities, and good judgment have combined to make me one of the rich men of this rich country. I have arrived at the stage at which my wealth accumulates almost automatically, and for many months now I have been turning over in my mind the question—What

2

shall I do with it ? How can I best fulfil my youthful resolve ?

S. Bravo, old fellow. I congratulate you. I had supposed you had gone over to the Philistines and sold your birthright for a mess of pottage. I can't tell you how delighted I am to find I was mistaken.

P. Thanks. But I want more from you than congratulations. I have persuaded you to come down here, because I want your advice. I want to take up our old discussions. I want you to advise me, to help me to make use of my wealth. You have spent thirty years in studying human nature and society. You have made a name for yourself in these studies. I want you to tell me whether, in the light of all your thinking and knowledge, you still have any of your old faith in the power of intellect and the good will to promote human welfare. Have you been disillusioned ? Are you content to support your family respectably, to bear an honoured name in the academic world, to add a little to scientific knowledge, and then to pass away with the vague hope that things will come right somehow, if only science progresses ? Have not the terrible events of the last few years taught you that the increasing control of the physical resources of the world which science brings does but add to the difficulties and dangers of mankind ? Isn't it clear now that civilization is in danger of destroying itself by the very means which science has so triumphantly provided ? Is not the fate of Germany,

3

its moral degradation, its political disorder, its economic chaos, is not all this a terrible warning? Does it not show that things of the sort that you and I have been doing since our college days are in themselves futile to save the world, or even to make it a better place than we found it? Germany excelled in our two lines of work, in economic development, the development of big business, and in the organized pursuit of science; and see what a mess she has made of her affairs. Her people were the most instructed, the best organized for peace and for war; her cities were excellently administered; her hospitals, her schools and universities were models for the whole world; her agriculture was scientific; only her churches were decaying. Does not the recent history of Germany show us only too clearly that all the things our philanthropists aim at, hygienic conditions, universal education, including popular interest in art and music, a rising standard of life, abolition of poverty, universal suffrage, that all these good things will not suffice to secure the moral health of a nation? Doesn't it look as though the mechanism of civilization which men have built up were getting too big and complicated for their control? When I contemplate putting my money into the promotion of any philanthropic scheme, the question rises in my mind—Will it do any good in the end? Won't it merely accelerate the process of increasing the scale and complexity of the mechanism of civilization?

S. I agree with you and I sympathize with you

in your perplexity. The example of other rich men who have tried to make their wealth serve mankind is not altogether encouraging. Carnegie's many millions are already beginning to seem a mere drop in the ocean. It is possible to doubt whether the world has been appreciably benefited by his gifts. Mr. Rockefeller has founded a great University and a great medical research institution. But the country can well afford to make and support its own universities ; and it is thought by some of my friends that the existence of large endowed research corporations has great drawbacks, even from the limited point of view of increase of knowledge.

Clearly, what you have to seek is some way of using your money which will fulfil two conditions : first, it must bring lasting benefit to mankind ; secondly, it must be of a kind which a rich democratic country will hardly adopt as a public measure.

P. Yes, you define my wishes exactly. I don't want merely to put a plaster on some local sore, to run soup-kitchens for starving millions, or maternity homes for deserving maidens. If there is no prospect that mankind, or some part of it, will achieve something more satisfactory than our present industrial civilization, then I would say, the more millions that starve, the better ; and the less maternity, the sooner this miserable race of men will come to an end.

S. I see you are not an easy-going optimist. But I agree with you. You and your like should not devote your wealth to the applying of social plasters ; nor should you give it for the support of institutions of the kind which should be and are supported by public funds. In the latter case your gifts would merely diminish in a hardly appreciable degree the rate of taxation throughout the country, and in a country so wealthy as this the effect would be hardly worth considering.

P. Well, you seem to have closed all possible roads for me. Is it really impossible to use great wealth to secure great and permanent goods ? I have seen that proposition laid down most emphatically. But I have not been able to bring myself to accept it ; and it is just because I don't see my way out of the difficulty that I am asking your advice. The people who make that statement are, I take it, the socialists or communists, those who think that all will be well if only private property can be abolished. And, upon my word, unless it is possible to find a way of spending wealth well, I don't see how its accumulation by individuals is to be justified. And yet, if we had a thorough-going communism, what would be the result ? The masses of the people, especially the lowest strata of unskilled workers, would breed enormously, and this great country after a few generations would be filled by hundreds of millions of low grade population ; we should become a second India. The game wouldn't be worth the candle.

S. I agree again. In that last remark you come near the essential problem. The only lasting benefit that can be conferred on mankind is the improvement of human qualities. Our social theorists propose all sorts of transformations of social and national organization, in the belief that mankind only needs to live under some particular form of ideal organization of society in order to be for ever happy. The truth is that forms of organization matter little; the all important thing is the quality of the matter to be organized, the quality of the human beings that are the stuff of our nations and societies. Under the best possible organization of society, civilization will decay and go to pieces if the quality of its human stuff is poor. Under the most anomalous and imperfect social forms, men will thrive and civilization will advance and improve itself, if the quality of its human stuff is sufficiently good. This is true on both the small and the large scale. The finest institutions will work miserably in incapable hands. Whereas if your population is of sufficiently good quality, morally and intellectually, any institution will work tolerably; and in the extreme case, institutions and organizations, governments and churches may all be decently interred in favour of a complete anarchy.

P. Ah! I see where you are leading me. I begin to remember some wild scheme you talked about in our college days. An island to be called Eugenia, wasn't it, devoted to the production of supermen? It seemed to me, I remember, the wildest romantic nonsense. I didn't believe you were serious about it. Don't tell me that you are still hugging that fantastic notion in your middle-aged bosom.

S. Yes, indeed I am. Thirty years of study of man, of his history and institutions, have only confirmed my youthful conviction that such a scheme is profoundly worth while, that it is practicable ; that the world is ripe for it, and needs it more urgently with every year that passes.

P. But look at the history of all such Utopian schemes. They have all fizzled out, or been converted to ordinary humdrum industrial communities after a very short time.

S. Yes, but they have all been run on wrong principles. You cannot argue that, because various imperfectly designed schemes of human betterment have failed, therefore every such scheme must fail. We are only now acquiring the knowledge that is essential for the wise designing of any such scheme. I only ask you to let me outline my plan and give me the benefit of your criticism as we go along.

P. Very well, I'm ready to listen and play the critic. It's the least I can do in return for your willingness to advise me in my perplexity.

S. I begin then by stating the principles on which Eugenia is to be founded. Civilizations decay because they die off at the top ; because, as they become increasingly complex, they cease to produce in sufficient numbers men and women of the moral and intellectual calibre needed for their support. So long as a nation produces in each generation a fair number of persons of first rate calibre, it can carry an enormous tail, without fatal decline. But the number of such persons tends to become not only relatively, but absolutely fewer with each generation ; because civilized societies breed from the bottom and die off at the top. I don't stop to substantiate this generalization. The evidence on which it is based is overwhelming. Instead, I will prescribe you a course of reading which will convince you of its truth.

The supply of persons of first-rate calibre can only be maintained by the fruitful mating of persons of superior strains. At present, as in all highly civilized societies, such persons tend to be absolutely or relatively infertile. Eugenia is a scheme for bringing persons of such strains together in fertile union which will give to the world an increasing number of persons of similar calibre.

P. Then you are going to institute the human stud-farm *à la* Plato. Seeing that his scheme has been before the world more than 2,000 years, why trouble to advocate it once more ?

S. Not so fast. Plato's scheme involved the destruction of the family, the denial of conjugal affection and parental responsibility. No scheme which ignores the strongest tendencies of human nature can hope to succeed. Eugenia will avoid this fundamental error. It will be founded on the cult of the family. Its religion will be something like ancestor worship, tempered by a reverence for the progeny, and a great faith in their value to mankind. It is to be a place in which persons of

9

superior strains shall come together in marriage and, under ideal conditions, produce the largest number of children compatible with the perfect strength and health of all concerned. It is to be an endogamous community, recruited by the admission of most carefully selected members from without, and improved by the rejection or extrusion of any of its native members who fail to come up to its standards of quality.

P. Then you propose to impoverish the rest of the world by bringing together in this community all its choicest spirits ; no doubt in some such way an ideal community might be achieved. But it would be at the cost of the rest of the world. The essential selfishness of such a scheme condemns it to failure.

S. You are going too fast again. Eugenia is not to be ruled by a selfish regard for itself. It will be animated by the spirit of world-service. Its children will be brought up with the noble ambition to serve the world. They will be aristocrats, but their tradition will be *Noblesse oblige*. The community will be a closed one only for the purposes of marriage and education. Membership in the community will be attained in every case by formal admission, after fullest inquiry into the family history and intellectual and moral qualifications of each candidate. The advantages of membership, the attractions of life in Eugenia, the privileges of participation in its exalted aims, will no doubt attract many candidates from the outer world ;

and the best of these will be admitted. But, once it has become a "going concern," Eugenia will recruit its citizens largely from the children born within its borders. Such children will not become citizens by right of birth alone. They too will attain membership only by formal admission. At the age of seventeen years they will become eligible ; it may be supposed that the great majority of them will desire to become citizens, and that of these the majority again will not fail to satisfy the strict requirements of family and personal qualifications laid down by the fundamental laws of Eugenia.

P. Then, if Eugenia is to be a closed community only as regards marriage, it will not require to be a community dwelling within a territorial boundary. Its members may live where they please.

S. Yes and No. Eugenia must certainly have its own well-defined territory, a homeland over which it must exercise complete authority. To that question we will come back presently. At this point I want to define the relations of the members to the homeland. Since the people of Eugenia are to serve the world, they will be free to come and go, to dwell in other lands and to take up any honourable calling in those other lands. The only essential requirement is that they shall spend the years from five to twenty mainly, if not wholly, within the borders of Eugenia. After being educated in the family, in school, and in college, the young people will be encouraged to complete their education in the great universities of the world ; only after doing so will they decide whether they will return to take up their life-work in the homeland or enter upon careers in some other country. And those who choose the latter course will not thereby sacrifice their membership. It will only be required of them that they marry within the community, that their homes shall be in Eugenia, and that their children shall be educated there. The relations of such members to the homeland may be illustrated by pointing to the relations of Indian Civil Servants to England. The Indian Civil Service has been a *corps d'élites* of Englishmen, who have accomplished one of the greatest tasks of recorded history, living and working far from their homeland. But they have not ceased to be Englishmen in the fullest sense of the word. They have married English women, their children have been brought up in England, their homes have been in England ; and to those homes they have returned, when their years of service in India have been completed.

P. That's all very well. But the parallel fails in one important point. Your Englishman in India does not want to marry an Indian woman. But your young Eugenians will go among people of their own race and of similar civilization. They will meet attractive persons, will fall in love and will marry and so be lost to Eugenia.

S. It is true that we shall probably lose a certain number of our young people in that way. But Eugenia can afford it, and that will be one of the principal ways in which she will be of service to the world at large. Every year she will contribute in this way to the population of other countries a number of splendid specimens of humanity ; perfect in body, of excellent moral disposition and character, and outstanding intellectual capacity. But we may safely anticipate that we shall retain enough of the best to maintain the numbers and the quality of the community. The young people of Eugenia will be encouraged to look forward to early marriage, and they will not be prevented from doing so by economic or prudential anxieties. Every member will know that all his or her children, born from a lawful wedlock with another Eugenian, will be amply provided for and given the best opportunities for bodily and mental development that the world can provide. We may confidently expect that, before going abroad in the early twenties to complete their education, very many will be already engaged, and many even married. They will have been led to see that early marriage and the production of many children is their greatest privilege, at once their highest duty and their best guarantee of happiness. May we not hope that, under such favourable conditions, families ranging from five to ten children will be the rule rather than the exception, and that Eugenia will swarm with beautiful, strong, and perfect children, the delight and pride of their parents and the hope of the world.

P. But how about the women folk ? We are told that the greatly restricted family, which has become the rule among the professional classes and the better-class artisans in all civilized countries, is mainly due to the repugnance of educated women to become mere bearers of children and domestic drudges. Will not the highly educated young women of Eugenia take the same view and follow the same practice ?

S. Undoubtedly some may do so, some in whom the maternal instinct is weak or who for any other reason fail to absorb the ideals of Eugenia. And these will go out into the world and will not return. But the moral atmosphere in which the girls grow up, and the high esteem in which parenthood will be held, the appeal to all that is best in them, will prepare the majority of them to face with enthusiasm the sufferings, the trials, the sorrows and the joys of motherhood. And as for the domestic drudgery, the whole plan of life in Eugenia will be directed to diminish to the utmost the more mechanical and menial of the domestic tasks. The mother of a large family will be aided in a hundred ways, not only by perfection of household arrangements, but by having helpers who will find their highest happiness in such work. Grandmothers, widows, spinsters, all the women who have no young children of their own to care for, will give at least a part of their time to helping the mothers. And so the young mother, instead of being worn down to premature old age by anxiety and drudgery, will find abundant helpers, educated gentlewomen like herself, to whom she can entrust the partial care of her brood with perfect confidence.

14

INTRODUCTION

P. I begin to think there may be some sense in this fantastic scheme of yours. Assuming that you have secured a fine stock of human beings to begin with, you count on their multiplying at a natural rate under the favourable moral and material conditions you hope to provide ; from this natural increase you discard constantly the least fit by denying them membership in your community ; and you seek further to improve the stock by admitting from time to time a certain number of highly selected persons.

S. Yes, that's the essence of the scheme. It is to secure all the advantages of a most rigid selection, not by the cruel methods of nature, whose great instrument is death or the selective death-rate ; but by a purely beneficent selection, which substitutes for the death penalty merely deprivation of the right to marry within the community, or, more strictly, deprivation of the right to remain within the community to all those who undertake marriage or procreation in defiance of its laws. And by admitting new members selected from the whole world according to the strictest principles, the immense benefits of rigid selection within the stock may be indefinitely augmented. Every biologist will tell you that, if such a scheme can be worked for a few generations, you can count upon producing a remarkably fine stock. Whether we can hope to secure in this way the production of many men and women of the first order of intellect, actual giants or geniuses, that is a further question, the answer to which is open to debate. But there is no room for doubt that we may expect to have a stock almost every child in which will be fitted to attain eminence in some walk of life and to render great services to his fellow-men.

P. Well, I'll grant, for the purpose of this discussion, that you may fairly anticipate this magnificent result if, as you said, the scheme can be worked. But what a large " IF " ! How are you going to start it ? How bring together your choice spirits, and the new Adams and the new Eves ? And if once started, how can you hope to guarantee it against the fate that has swiftly overtaken every other community of cranks, namely, dissension and dissolution.

S. I grant you that most of the many " crank " communities have had short lives and have been fit objects for the world's derision. But let me point out that there is at least one exception, namely, the Mormon community. All those others, from Brook Farm to the Oneida Settlement, have suffered the fate they deserved, the fate that might have been confidently foretold by anyone with a little knowledge of human nature ; for they ignored or defied the fundamentals of human nature. The Mormons, on the other hand, have flourished greatly and have achieved a community which in very many respects outshines all competitors. That is because their fundamental principle was in accordance with an outstanding, an undeniable fact of human nature, the polygamous tendency of the human male. Now, as I have said, Eugenia is to be founded on monogamy. For, though man is polygamous, woman is not. Woman, when her nature is unperverted, prefers to have her own man and her own home and her own children about her. And, unless it could be shown that the biological welfare of the group absolutely demands polygamy, the ideal State must demand of man that suppression of his polygamous tendency which the happiness of women, the stability of the family, and his own spiritual welfare alike require.

P. I had forgotten the Mormons. I admit they are an exception to the rule. But let me hear how you propose to initiate your great experiment.

S. This is where you come in with your millions. Other rich men have given vast sums to endow universities, libraries, research institutions, peace prizes, and so forth ; none of these, as you yourself have so clearly seen, promises any lasting benefit. I offer you now a means of applying your wealth in a way which far surpasses all these in its promise. If you adopt my plan, you may feel a reasonable confidence in the attainment of great results. And when at some future time you and Andrew Carnegie look down upon this world from some distant star, you will be able to point out to him with legitimate pride the sons and daughters of Eugenia, and unroll before his envious eyes the record of their great achievements.

The first essential is a suitable territory. An island would have many advantages. But whether an island or not, it should be not less than 500 square miles in extent, and might with advantage be as large as 10,000 square miles. It should have a white man's climate and a reasonably fertile soil. It should have some natural beauty. The more diversified and beautiful its natural features, the better it will serve our purpose. There you are to found a great university for both sexes, the nucleus of a group of great professional schools and centres of post-graduate study and research.

By offering adequate salaries and ideal conditions of living and working, you will attract a brilliant staff of instructors. In appointing them regard will be paid, not only to the personal qualifications of applicants, but also to their family histories ; and in the cases of those who are married, the personal and family qualifications of wife or husband will be taken into account. In other words, your instructors will be persons not obviously disqualified for membership in the community, but rather *prima facie* qualified for admission. After some years of service, the question of their admission to full membership will arise, and each case will be carefully considered on its merits. He (or she) who does not desire full membership, or has not the necessary qualifications, will resign his post and transfer his talents to some other sphere. Those who desire full membership and who have the required qualities will be solemnly admitted. Whether they will suffer rites and mysteries at their initiation, the taste of the community may decide ;

but some formal and public recognition of their admission must be made. In this way you will secure a nucleus of Eugenians. This nucleus will grow rapidly by natural generation, for marriage and parenthood will be held in high honour. And everything will be done to make smooth the path of family life. The brilliant young teacher or writer or scientist will not be torn by the conflict between his ambition, his desire to do great work, his sense of the supreme value of the intellectual life, and his natural desire for marriage, a home and a family. In this happy land duty and inclination will coincide ; the two chief goods of human life will not be incompatible. Failure to marry and sterility after marriage will be serious bars to the continuance of tenure of position ; the bachelor and the childless will enjoy no economic advantages over those whose quivers are full.

And this nucleus will be recruited by many of the best among the students who will flock to your university from all parts of the world, attracted by its unique advantages. These also will be selected from the swarm of applicants with due regard to racial and family as well as to personal qualifications. And, when they shall have passed one, two, or more years within the walls of your university, they will become eligible for membership in the community. They will probably have to serve a probationary period after election.

P. Then you propose to create a community of lily-fingered scholars, living on imported tinned meats, jam and pickles, a swarm of parasites, not one of whom could do a decent day's work, or earn an honest living, if thrown on his own resources.

S. My dear sir, when did you acquire this exaggerated respect for the horny-handed sons of toil ? Eugenia will be in a certain sense and degree parasitic ; just as every university, every institution of the higher learning, of art or of science, is parasite, as you and I are parasite ; in so far, namely as the Eugenians will not be wholly or chiefly employed in securing the primary necessities of life. But like those other institutions, and in a far higher degree, Eugenia will justify its parasitism by the great services it will render to the world. Symbiosis, rather than parasitism, is the right word to use in describing its relations to the world at large. But granted a partial dependence upon the outer world as inevitable, Eugenia will not forget how Adam delved and Eve span. Every child will be taught a trade, will learn how to use his hands as well as his head ; and, when he grows to man's estate, he will not need to relieve the tedium of his leisure with interminable rounds of golf or sets of tennis. Games will not be taboo ; but every man will be expected to devote a part of his time to practical labour of an immediately useful kind. The professor of astronomy will milk the cows, the expert in chemistry will handle a Fordson tractor with a satisfying efficiency, the social anthropologist will look after the bee-hives, while the professor of fine arts or philosophy may be expected to cultivate his sense of humour by attending to the pigs. I think we may hope that, when once the little State shall have got into smooth running order, it will become nearly self-supporting, will rely more and more on its own economic activities and marketable products and less upon its endowments.

P. And how about the political status of Eugenia ? Do you see it under its own flag, maintaining its own army and navy, and sending out its ambassadors to lie abroad ?

S. No, certainly not. It is clear, I think, that it will need the protection of a great Power, and that it must fly either the Stars and Stripes or the Union Jack. It might well be a territory of U.S.A., or a British Protectorate. Sarawak might serve as a model in this respect ; a little country, about as big physically as England, ruled most happily by an Englishman and a small handful of colleagues, but protected from aggression by all the might of the British Empire, while free from all interference by the British Government.

P. Then Eugenia is to be as nearly as possible an independent State, having its own laws and political constitution.

S. Yes, that is the most desirable status for it. Its constitution might be very simple and the laws few. It should approximate to that happy condition dreamed of by the philosophic anarchists, in which laws and courts of justice and police for their enforcement are all outgrown. But I recognize that it may be difficult to secure for it a suitable territory not already subject to the laws of one of the Great Powers, and I think you might be content to see it subject to the laws of either U.S.A. or Great Britain. I can see no harm in that, so long as the community owns and controls its territory. In the beginning its territory and public buildings and financial resources should be controlled by a board of trustees ; which board might well be recruited as time goes on in accordance with the principles of representative democracy.

P. If your plan is successful and your Eugenians multiply freely as you wish them to do, they will double their numbers every twenty years or so ; and so your little State will soon be threatened by the spectre that dogs every successful State, the spectre of over-population ; quite apart from those desirable new recruits whom you design to attract from all parts of the world.

S. There again Eugenia will be in a peculiarly happy position. The more her people multiply, the more she will feel she is playing her part in the world well and truly. As soon as the community shall have attained to such a number as seems the optimum for her territory, she will need to retain in her service only two members of each family of children, the others, three, four, five, or more, will be launched upon the world to seek their fortunes. They will go out, splendidly equipped in mind and body and with noble ideals of service, to play their part in the great world. No doubt many a one will tear himself away with a heavy heart, just as many a youth has found it difficult to leave the happy scenes of his college life. But, the step once taken, they will soon make for themselves honourable careers. They will be the salt of the earth, leaders in all the professions, bound together and to their Alma Mater by memories of their happy youth and their sense of their part in the realization of a great ideal. And this surplus increase of population will give to Eugenia the opportunity of a sustained and stringent selection which, if wisely used, will result in a continued evolution of human qualities to which our reason can foresee no limits and which our imagination cannot depict.

P. I foresee that your plan will require all of the fifty millions sterling of which you spoke at the outset of our talk, if it is to be adequately launched and endowed. I must put it before some of my fellow dyspeptics who, like myself, can't stomach all their wealth. Meantime, do you work out your scheme in greater detail and subject it for criticism to your colleagues. Get together a group of biologists, psychologists, sociologists, and people of that kind, and let them pull it to pieces if they can. Then we will meet again and have another talk on ways and means. But one last objection before we turn in. Obviously your scheme will encounter the derision of all Philistines. I don't know that that need trouble you. But is there in the world any considerable number of persons of the right sort who would uproot themselves from the well-trodden pathways of national life in order to venture their lives in the crazy barque imagined by you? I mean is there any hope that a group of reasonably well-endowed persons could be got together to initiate your colony? Won't you have to be content with a collection of cranks and failures, ill-balanced visionaries and discontented paranoids seeking refuge from a world that has proved too hard for them?

S. I haven't the least misgiving on that score. There are thousands of young people asking themselves at this moment—What is best worth doing? How can I devote myself to some course of life that is really worth while? You and I, my dear fellow, when we burned with the ardent desire to do some good in the world, were not rare exceptions. If only you and your fellow dyspeptics will do your part, Eugenia can be made so attractive, so appealing to all that is best, all that is idealistic in human nature, that we shall practically be able to select our members from the whole human race. Candidates for admission will surge around our doors. The deliberate founding of a colony is not a new and unheard-of proposition. Think of Greece, of Rome, of England. Perpetual colonization has been the essence of the history of the Nordic race. That fine race seems in fact incapable of surviving, when it ceases to migrate and colonize. It is one of the virtues of Eugenia that it offers the prospect of saving a remnant of that disappearing race, of perpetuating the stock and restoring and perhaps even enhancing its ancient virtue. But I don't want to raise the racial question, with all its inevitable prejudices. The effects of race-blending and the many allied problems of human biology will be a principal field of research in the University of Eugenia. We may confidently expect that this department will attract the most brilliant of our students. Historical study will no longer mean minute research into ancient charters and forgotten personalities, it will be a sub-department of Anthropology. The science of man will for the first time receive adequate recognition, that is to say, it will dominate the scene. To it all other sciences will be duly subordinated ; and they will be valued and studied in proportion as they contribute to the solution of its supremely important problems. For underlying all the activities of Eugenia will be the conviction that, if the human race is to have a future that we can contemplate without horror and despair, it can achieve such a future only by deliberately assuming the control of its own destiny.

CHAPTER I

IN this book I propose to discuss a most
difficult and obscure problem; not because
I have any new or startling conclusions to
announce, but because the facts and reflections
I wish to put before the reader have urgent
bearing upon many problems of private conduct
and public policy. The importance of the topic
is very great for all peoples, but for the British
people at the present time it seems to me to over-
shadow and dwarf every other that any man of
science could propose for its consideration. The
British nation has steadily increased its power and
influence in the world during some three centuries
of expansion. Now, emerging triumphant from
the greatest struggle in which it has ever taken
part, it seems to stand among the shattered nations
stronger, relatively at least, than ever before. Only
the American nation now stands in the same rank
in respect of control of the material bases of
civilization, of prestige, and of capacity for shaping
the future of Western civilization. The history of
the expansion of Britain, in spite of some dark
chapters, may justly inspire every citizen of the
British Empire with pride, and with a great hope

for the part it may yet play in the world in co-operation with the American people, so closely allied with it in blood, in traditions, and in ideals. Yet both these great nations are threatened by an insidious danger which, if we cannot learn to cope with it, will bring our brightest hopes to nothingness, and render our ideals merely the fleeting visions of a golden age that is past.

The great increase of knowledge which we owe to the scientific labours of the nineteenth century has put us, the bearers of the civilization of the twentieth century, in a position that has no precedent, a position profoundly different from that of any of the great civilizations of the past. The Romans, the Greeks, the Persians, the Egyptians, the Babylonians were surrounded by unknown possibilities ; their vision was confined to a small area of the earth and to their own immediate past. To foresee their future or to control it was for them wholly impossible. How different is our position ! We have mapped the whole earth ; we know its status and relations among the other heavenly bodies ; we can describe, in a general way, its past history during many millions of years ; we understand in some degree all the physical energies, and can in a large measure control them and bend them to the service of mankind. All the races of men are known to us. There remains no great reservoir of humankind which may issue from some uncharted region to overwhelm and destroy our civilization. And, most important of all, we are beginning to

28

understand something of the nature of man, something of the history of the development of the species, something of our bodily frame and mental powers, and of the long process by which our intellectual and moral culture has been achieved.

The Great War has given us one new item of knowledge which completes our assurance that we, the heirs of Western civilization, hold its destiny in our hands to make or mar. Before the war it was an open question whether civilized man, bred largely in towns to sedentary modes of life, could sustain the hardships and strains of prolonged warfare; whether, in a clash of arms against some more primitive people, we might not be overborne and swept away for sheer lack of nerve, of animal courage; whether our town-bred bespectacled young men, their imaginations quickened by education, and all unused to physical hardship, pain, and bloodshed, might not shrink and crumble when brought face to face with the horrors of war. But in the terrible years we have lived through we have seen regiments of cockneys from the London suburbs, and of Lancashire lads drawn from the mills and factories of the world's greatest industrial hive, distinguish themselves by gallantry and by patient courage in the field. These men have remained resolute and cheerful under a strain of warfare which, in respect of its horrors, its intense physical and emotional shocks, and the long continuance of the strain, has far surpassed every previous and more primitive warfare. We know now that civilization and culture, even in their worst forms, do not necessarily sap the moral energies of men ; rather, we know that trained intelligence and disciplined will can withstand the extreme horrors of war far better than the cruder more animal courage of the primitive hunter and warrior.

Our civilization stands, then, in this position of immense advantage as compared with all civilizations of the past. And on the British and American peoples lies the responsibility for its future in a greater degree than on any others ; because they have at their command, in a higher degree than any others, all the resources, material and spiritual, from which our civilization proceeds.

I will state concisely the thesis which I shall develop and attempt to prove in the following pages. Looking back over the history of mankind, we see that it consists in the successive rise and decay of great civilizations borne by different peoples in various parts of the earth. I need not enumerate these ; their names are familiar to you. The facts have been insisted upon by many writers ; they have been displayed by none more clearly than by Professor Flinders Petrie in his " Revolutions of Civilization." They are summed up in the familiar phrase, " cycles of civilization." They are briefly as follows. We see again and again a people in some favoured area of the earth's surface slowly build up a great and complex civilization, incorporating essential elements of culture which it has acquired from some older civilization, adding to them and moulding them into harmony with its own genius and special needs. For many centuries the slow process of upbuilding, growth, and enrichment goes on. Then comes an arrest, and, usually after a comparatively short period, the whole complex organism decays and plunges more or less rapidly downward from the height it had attained. In some cases the decay has gone so far that nothing remains of the people and its culture beyond a few mounds of earth and broken brick. In others the people has continued to exist, but stagnant and inert, contributing nothing further to the progress of mankind, retaining little or nothing of what was most admirable in its period of ascent and greatness.

It is as though each such people, having been projected upon its upward path by some great force, maintains its ascending movement until its momentum is spent, then falls back to earth, a mere mass of human clay, undistinguished above others by any power to create, to progress, or in any way rise above the common level of mankind. If we seek a phrase which will convey most concisely the nature of this recurring process, the process which has been denoted by the phrase "revolutions or cycles of civilization," we may, I suggest, best describe it as "the parabola of peoples." For the course of the rise and fall of a people tends to resemble the trajectory of a stone thrown obliquely upward from the hand, a long ascending curve, an almost flat summit, and a steep decline.

Many speculations have been provoked by the contemplation of this recurring phenomenon. The first response of the mind is to ask—Is this inevitable, is this parabola the expression of some inescapable law of nature? Are we also destined to follow the same curve and, sooner or later, to plunge downward to stagnation or decay? Or may we, by taking thought, hope to escape the common fate of all our predecessors? Can we establish our course so securely that our descendants may continue to progress, for an indefinitely long period, in art and science and social organization, attaining heights of power, security, and happiness unimaginable by us?

In order to answer these questions, we must have some understanding of the causes of the rise and fall of the curve of civilization. The answers that have been suggested fall into two main classes : first, the answer implied by the economic interpretation of history ; secondly, the anthropological answer. The former would see the essential factors in changes of climate, discoveries of new sources of wealth or of energy, or the opening up of new regions of the earth and the consequent shiftings of trade routes. The anthropological theory regards all such economic factors as of but subsidiary importance. It points out that peoples which were destined to climb the curve have subdued and transformed the physical world to their needs or, if necessary, have sought out and ·conquered for themselves a more propitious habitat. It points to regions such as Mesopotamia and the Nile valley, where men have made the desert bloom with all that was needed as the physical basis of great civilizations. And it points to other great regions, such as Africa south of the Sahara, and South and North America, regions which are richest in all that man needs and which nevertheless produced hardly more than savagery or barbarism, while Europe and Asia saw the rise and fall of many civilizations. It asserts also that in such regions as Mesopotamia and Egypt there have been no great changes (save such as man himself has produced) which could account for the rise or fall of their peoples. It points to the fact that the Roman Empire, which for four hundred years controlled the resources of the fairest regions of Europe, Northern Africa, and Asia, levying tribute upon all the known world, went down beneath the assault of the barbarians from the North, without any great change of economic conditions that can be assigned as a cause. Such instances show that the economic factors are of secondary importance ; they show that the most favourable area can become the seat of a great civilization only when it is occupied by a people more capable than most of profiting by its geographic advantages ; and that these advantages will not avail to save a people from decay, if and when it loses its natural superiority.

One anthropologic theory has been widely accepted

3

as accounting for the decay of peoples. Leaving the problem of their ascent untouched, it asserts that peoples grow old, just as men and animals do, and that they must as inevitably decline in vigour after a certain age. It cannot be too strongly insisted that this fatalistic theory is utterly unfounded, if it is offered as anything more than a descriptive formula.

Professor Flinders Petrie, who has brought out so clearly the facts we are considering, and who points out that the period of the cycle or parabola has approximated in many instances to one thousand eight hundred years, advances a theory which claims to explain both the rise and the fall of the curve. He supposes that every cycle is initiated by a biological blending of two races; that this gives to the blended stock a new energy which carries it up the scale of civilization; that, after about one thousand eight hundred years, this effect is exhausted and that, in consequence of loss of vigour, decline inevitably sets in.

There may be some truth in this view as regards the initiation of the rise of a civilization. There is some evidence that the crossing of closely related stocks does conduce to increase of vigour and probably also to variability; and that these effects must be favourable to national progress seems obvious. Vigour, energy of mind and body, is certainly an all-important factor, without which all other natural endowments and advantages will effect little. And variability of the stock would

34

seem to be a necessary condition of the production of the persons of exceptional endowments without whom a nation can neither rise in the scale of civilization nor maintain a great position.

But, as regards the decline of peoples, Petrie's theory seems to contain less of truth. The old view that inbreeding necessarily results in degeneration has been much blown upon of late. Facts are accumulating which seem to show that very close inbreeding is compatible with continued and even increased vigour of the stock.

Now, it is this second part of the problem in which we are practically interested. We belong to a stock which has produced a great civilization, one which seems to be still on the ascending part of its curve. Our concern, our responsibility, is to maintain if possible that ascending curve, or at least to postpone as long as possible the onset · of the period of decline, if that, in truth, must inevitably come. And there are not lacking indications that our Western civilization may already have reached its climax, may even now be sliding down the curve of decline. For we must not allow ourselves to be dazzled by the material achievements of the recent past. In trying to estimate our position, we must have regard to moral and intellectual achievements of kinds less easily appreciated than the aeroplane and the big gun, the submarine and the poison-gas.

It is true that we have obtained a wonderful command over the physical energies of the world ;

but if we have not, individually and collectively as nations, the wisdom, the patience, the self-control to direct these immense energies conformably to high moral ideals, our tampering with them will but hasten our end, will but plunge us the more rapidly down the slope of destruction. There is but too good ground for the fear that our knowledge has outrun our wisdom, that, though we have learned to exploit the physical energies of the world, we have not the wisdom and morality effectively to direct them for the good of mankind.

Leaving, then, the obscure problem of the origins of civilizations and of the causes of the ascent of peoples, I wish to concentrate your attention upon the more urgent and practically important problem of the causes or conditions that bring about their decline. In respect of this great problem, my thesis is that the anthropological theory is the true one, *that the great condition of the decline of any civilization is the inadequacy of the qualities of the people who are the bearers of it.*

This inadequacy may be one of two kinds; or it may be, perhaps generally has been, of both kinds. Inadequacy of the one kind may result from the increase of complexity of the environment which accompanies the rise of civilization, which is, in fact, an inevitable and necessary feature of it. Without change of the essential qualities of a people, those qualities may become relatively inadequate to the support of its civilization; just because advancing civilization makes, with every step of progress, greater demands upon its bearers. Let me illustrate by reference to three great features which, in various degrees, appear in all civilizations. First, increasing control of natural resources gives men leisure and opportunity to seek relaxation and amusement. Now leisure and amusement are most dangerous things, as some of us know. Few men are capable of using leisure and of choosing their amusements entirely wisely, and some men are quite incapable of doing so. Well, civilization inevitably lays upon great masses of men this responsibility. How do they respond to it ? We know how in the great age of Rome the circus, the combat of gladiators and of wild beasts, and the chariot races became the passionate delight of the multitude. We know how many forms of luxury, wines, perfumes, foods, baths, slaves, with resulting habits of indulgence, were introduced from all parts of the world. Under such complexities of environment many men who, under simpler conditions, would have lived solid, useful, and happy lives, became enervated, their interests and leisure increasingly absorbed in these useless if not actually harmful amusements.

Secondly, the increase of complexity of personal relations tends also to demand ever higher qualities from the persons concerned. Consider the relations of employer and workman. In the days of slavery, whether in Greece or Rome or Virginia, how simple were the qualities required for the satisfactory working of the institution,

37

the relation ! The owner of an estate worked by slaves had only to be an intelligent and kind-hearted man in order to be surrounded by happy faithful workers, a benevolent autocrat in the midst of grateful and devoted followers. And in the intermediate stage of small farming and small industry, where the employer is in close personal contact with all his men, a small dose of kindliness and good sense goes a long way to the maintenance of satisfactory relations. But to-day, in our industrial world, what great demands are made on the qualities of the employer ! How patient, how understanding, how far-sighted, how humane he must be, if he is to avoid bitter strife with his work-people !

Thirdly, and perhaps most important, the increased intercourse between peoples, which is a leading feature and condition of progressing civilization, inevitably weakens, when it does not altogether destroy, the influence of the customs and moral traditions by which our lives are guided. Instead of being moulded insensibly to conform to the customs and traditions which have sufficed to bring our forefathers safely through the perils of life, to guide them in the simpler environment of the past, we are confronted by ever more numerous possibilities of choice between rival customs and traditions and new beliefs and theories. We are called upon to choose wisely, to steer our course warily, among untried but perhaps attractive novelties, new religions, new social theories, new ethical precepts.

And the result of all this is inevitable ; it is the price that must be paid for progress ; not only do the customs and traditions to which each man adheres exert a less powerful sway over his conduct, but also the harmony of the society in which and by which he lives is weakened and disordered.

In these ways, and in many others, every advance of civilization makes greater demands upon the qualities of its bearers ; and it is, I think, obvious that in these respects our present civilization has surpassed all its predecessors, surpassed them in the opportunities for leisure and amusement, in the complexity of personal relations, in the variety of customs, traditions, beliefs, theories of conduct, with which we are brought in contact, all demanding on our part the exercise of a wisdom, a self-control, and a degree of devotion to a moral ideal, such as no previous civilization has required.

We are making great efforts to meet these demands, we are multiplying and improving our educational institutions ; and the rising generation seems to be responding, by making full use of the advantages provided for it. But there remains to be answered the all-important question—Is it possible, by improved and extended education, adequately to prepare the rising generations for the immense responsibilities they must bear ? Are their innate qualities such as will enable them to rise to the level required by the increasing complexity and difficulty of the tasks that will be laid upon them ? Will the human qualities which have carried our civilization upward to its present point of complexity —will they suffice to carry it further, or even to maintain it at its present level ?

That is a grave question. But a still graver question calls for our most earnest consideration, namely : Does not progressive civilization, while it makes ever greater demands on the qualities of its bearers, does it not tend to impair, has it not always in the past actually impaired, the qualities of the peoples on whom it makes these increasing demands ?

History and Anthropology seem to point to the same answer to this grave question—namely, to the positive answer. History seems to exhibit unmistakably this tendency of civilization to impair the qualities of its bearers ; and Anthropology shows us how and why it has so worked in the past and still is tending, perhaps more strongly than ever before, in this direction.

Here, then, is the anthropological theory of the decline of peoples :

Every human being, and therefore every community of human beings, every populace, inherits from its ancestry a stock of innate qualities which enable it to enjoy, to sustain, to promote a civilization of a certain degree of complexity. As civilization advances, it makes greater and greater demands on these qualities, requires their exercise and development in ever fuller degree, until it approaches a point at which its complexity outruns the possibilities of the innate qualities. At the same time it tends positively to impair those qualities ; so that, as the demands increase, the latent reserves of human quality are diminished. Therefore a time comes when the supply no longer equals the demand ; that moment is the culminating point of that civilization and of that people, the turning-point of the curve from which the downward plunge begins. This downward tendency may be gradual and difficult to discern at first ; but History seems to show that it is apt to be an accelerating process.

Anthropology is the latest and most backward of the sciences. The proper study of mankind is man. But how difficult is that study ! It is not very difficult to study the things that man has made, his languages, his arts, his manufactures, his social organizations, his achievements of all kinds. But how difficult to infer from these the nature of man's constitution ! How difficult to correlate any peculiarities in these products of his activities with any peculiarities of natural endowment ! The physical anthropologists have, during the last half century, accumulated a vast mass of data about certain of his bodily qualities —the proportions of his skull and other bones, the colour of his eyes, his stature, and his complexion and his hair. These data are of great value ; but they concern merely his material structure. It is the mental constitution of man, the varying sum of his mental qualities, that is alone of direct importance and with which we are concerned. The bodily peculiarities are of importance chiefly in so far as they may serve as indicators of mental qualities. It is this mental anthropology which is so difficult a study that it has only quite recently begun to take shape as a science, the science we call modern psychology. And that science is, accordingly, in a very rudimentary condition, hopeful and active, but still the scene of the most widely divergent views in respect of its fundamental questions. Especially as regards the innate basis of the human mind, we still have little light and much difference of opinion. Yet only knowledge of the innate basis of the mind will enable us to arrive at well-founded views, in face of the great problems of the rise and fall of nations.

No wonder, then, that, when these problems began to be actively debated early in the last century, there were acute differences of opinion, much error, and much false dogma. For not only was all such discussion carried on in the total absence of the necessary basis of knowledge, but it was a discussion in which the participants almost inevitably were moved by strong desires other than the desire for truth, in which judgment was distorted by strong prejudices and sentiments. The debate inevitably raised the question of the relative values of the human races, the superiority or inferiority of this race to that, of one people to another. In the absence of all certain knowledge of the fundamental facts, what hope was there that racial bias should be discounted and kept in check?

The story opens with the myth of the Aryan

42

race. This " race " was a phantasy erected by
racial prejudice on a basis of the study of languages.
Community of language was accepted, in the
face of all probability, as evidence of community
of race. And the learned world was convulsed
with controversies over the origin of the Aryans,
a race which had never existed. From the first,
racial prejudice was at work ; for the Aryans were
conceived as the race which had produced all that
was most esteemed in the culture of Europe and
of Asia ; and, from the first, the whole question
was confused by the search for the lost tribes of
Israel. The errors of this early stage of the discussion provoked some of the most influential writers
of the middle of last century to repudiate the notion
of differences of mental constitution between the
races of men. J. S. Mill declared : " Of all vulgar
modes of escaping from the consideration of the
effect of social and moral influences on the human
mind, the most vulgar is that of attributing the
diversities of conduct and character to inherent
natural differences." And he was followed by many
others. For at that time the prevailing view of the
human mind, of which Mill was the chief exponent,
was all against the assumption of racial differences ;
and the prevailing humanitarian sentiment, of which
also Mill was a leading exponent, made strongly
in the same direction. The psychology of that
time was the " Association psychology " that had
come down from Locke and Hume. It taught
that at birth the human mind is a blank sheet, and

the brain a structureless mass, lacking all inherent organization or tendencies to develop in this way or that ; a mere mass of undefined potentialities which, through experience, association, and habit, through education in short, could be moulded and developed to an unlimited extent and in any manner or direction.

There prevailed, therefore, at that time a profound belief in the unlimited power of education. J. S. Mill himself had been most carefully educated from his earliest years by his father ; and he attributed his own achievements in the intellectual sphere wholly to that fact, overlooking a still more important fact, namely, that he was the son of his father, a man of great intellectual vigour and capacity. Even those who perceived the truth that by education you cannot make every child into a great man, believed, nevertheless, that the educative process had only to be applied to some few successive generations, in order to raise any people or any human stock to an indefinite degree in the scale of intellectual and moral value.

Humanitarian sentiment worked powerfully in favour of this theory of the unlimited power of education. For there is something cold and cruel, something repugnant to the natural kindliness of the normal man, in the opposite theory, the theory that some men, and even whole races of men, are born incapable of being educated beyond a very modest level of intellectual and moral achievement. We should all like to agree with the member of the

44

British Parliament who, indignantly repudiating an aspersion cast upon some section of his countrymen, declared that " one man is as good as another —and a great deal better too, sometimes."

So striking are the immediate effects of education, and so strong is the influence of humanitarian feeling upon opinion, that this confidence in the unlimited power of education still prevails in the popular mind : it is, I think, the basis of much of the fine optimism with which the American people confronts its tasks, the implicit theory on which its practice is based.[1]

Yet, since the day of Mill, science has done much that saps this theory ; it has achieved new knowledge which, if it were generally understood, would go far to undermine the complacency with which the popular mind contemplates the future.

This new insight into the nature of man forbids us scornfully to set aside, as the vulgar errors of the " race-theorizers," all attempts to estimate the intrinsic values, the cultural potentialities, of different human stocks. It calls upon us to weigh the evidence most carefully and impartially, putting aside, as strictly as in us lies, both racial prejudice and humanitarian sentiment ; to recognize that, if Nature has made men of unequal value, the cruelty is hers, not ours, and that we do no wrong in ascertaining and recording the facts.

[1] For example, I am told by a prominent educationist that America is engaged in levelling up the Philippines to her own standards by instituting universal and compulsory schooling among them.

The framers of the Declaration of Independence of the United States of America embodied in it the celebrated proposition that " all men are created equal." There are two senses in which this sentence may be interpreted. It may be taken to mean that all men are equal in respect of their claims for justice, for humane treatment and the kindly feeling of their fellows, for opportunities to make the best of their powers of service and of happiness. On the other hand, it may be, and sometimes has been, taken to mean that all men are born with equal capacities for intellectual and moral development. There can be no doubt, I think, that the former interpretation is the true one. The untruth of the second interpretation is so obvious, and in all ages has been so obvious, that we do wrong to the great men who framed the proposition, if we assume that the second meaning was intended by them. In the former sense the proposition conveys a great moral truth and a moral ideal which all men can accept as a fundamental principle of conduct.

CHAPTER II

A BOUT the time at which J. S. Mill denounced the vulgar errors of the race-theorizers, and at which T. H. Buckle, the historian of civilization in Europe, claimed to show that the peoples of the various regions of the earth are moulded by their physical environments like so much soft clay, the theory of the all-importance of race took a new turn and gave rise to a school of thought which has flourished greatly, which still flourishes, and which has produced great and disastrous historical effects.

In 1854 Count Gobineau published his treatise on the "Inequality of the Races of Man," and thereby founded the German school of race-dogmatists, sometimes called the school of politico-anthropology. He announced to the world: "I have become convinced that everything in the way of human creation, science, art, civilization, all that is great and noble and fruitful on the earth, points toward a single source, is sprung from one and the same root, belongs only to one family, the various branches of which have dominated every civilized region of the world." This family

47

he asserted to be the Teutonic race. Gobineau's race-theory chimed so well with the political aspirations of the leaders of Germany that, with appropriate modification to the effect that the modern Germans are the purest representatives of the super-race, it became the official doctrine of that country. It was adopted and propagated assiduously by a multitude of men, both great and small. Richard Wagner was one of the ardent disciples of this school. Nietzsche's conception of a " great blond beast " of a superman gave the dogma a literary expression which profoundly influenced many young Germans. German anthropologists busied themselves to discover evidence in its support. H. S. Chamberlain, popularly known as the Kaiser's favourite anthropologist, gave it its most complete expression in his " Foundations of the 19th Century," a book which greatly influenced the Germans, from Wilhelm II downward. In these ways, by means of this conspiracy officially promoted for the perversion of the truth, the German people, docile as always to its elaborately organized system of official instruction, was persuaded to believe, against the evidence of most obvious facts, that it was the chosen people of the world. And the acceptance of this race-dogma did much to convince the leaders and the masses of the German people that they were morally justified in setting out in 1914 to exterminate their weaker neighbours as a first and necessary step to that world-rulership to which they believed themselves to be destined by Nature or by God. And the professors, if we may judge by many utterances, including the infamous manifesto signed by ninety-three of the most prominent of them, were just as suggestible and deluded as the masses. This dogma of the natural and predestined supremacy of the German people gave rise incidentally, but inevitably, to a polemic against the Jews, and greatly promoted the crusade of the Anti-Semites. For the Jews had long claimed to be the chosen people of the Lord ; and their remarkable persistence as a people, in spite of all adverse influences, and, it may be added, their remarkable achievements, lent some colour to this view. Thus the race-dogma accentuated racial hatred and international hostilities. Odious as all this was, it had one good effect. It stimulated some men, more especially a number of capable Jews, to examine in a critical spirit the evidence on which the race-dogma claimed to be founded.

Notable among these are Friedrich Hertz, author of " Modern Race Theories," and Ignaz Zollshan, whose book, " The Race Problem," published in 1909, is a critical examination of the German race-dogma and a temperate and successful defence of the racial value of the Jews. These writers had no difficulty in exposing to impartial readers the exaggerations and distortions of the German race-dogmatists. The logic of the latter was deplorable, and their disregard of facts was obvious to the most casual reader. It was their habit to discover some traces of physical qualities, such as tall stature, blue eyes, long heads, or fair hair, among whatever people had achieved any noteworthy work, and, taking this as evidence of some infusion of Germanic blood, to attribute the achievement of that people wholly to this alleged strain in the population concerned.

I will not delay to expose their methods and the falsity of their claims. I will merely point out that a less extreme and more defensible form of this race-theory still finds many supporters. Dr. C. Woodruff [1] and Mr. Madison Grant,[2] in America, De Lapouge[3] in France are examples. They claim an intrinsic and great superiority, not for the Germans or the Teutons, but for the Nordic race of Europe, which is represented in Germany, it is true, but not so strongly as in other areas. Anthropologists are now pretty well agreed that this Nordic race really did exist, and that, mixed in various proportions, its blood is still widely represented in various parts of the world. Without claiming for it any general innate superiority, we may fairly inquire whether it possessed and still exhibits any human qualities in peculiar degree or combination. But, before passing to examine the evidence for differences of natural endowment, let us glance at the arguments of those who to-day represent the school of Mill, denying all differences of mental endowment, or regarding them as so

[1] "The Expansion of Races."
[2] "The Passing of the Great Race."
[3] "Les Sélections Sociales."

slight as to be negligible factors in world-history.

Of the many critics of the race-dogmatists, I will cite only the names of M. J. Finot, author of " The Prejudices of Race," of Mr. J. M. Robert-son, the vindicator of Buckle, and of Mr. J. Oake-smith. Mr. Oakesmith's book on " Race and Nationality " (1919) is the latest important work on this side of the argument and well represents the rest. These authors, who deny all importance to racial composition and differences of innate endowment, may conveniently be classed over against their opponents, the race-dogmatists, as the " race-slumpers." It is characteristic of them that they in the main avoid the straight issue and content themselves with exposing the errors of the race-dogmatists. They make much of the undeniable truth that none of the civilized peoples of the world are of pure race, but rather are all alike the products of repeated blendings of races and peoples. They point out that, if any racial peculiarities of mental constitution exist, they are so obscure that no one has been able to define them and measure them, as the physical anthropologists have succeeded in defining and measuring certain physical qualities as indicators of race. They point to the fact that in many instances men born of primitive and even savage parents have shown themselves capable of acquir-ing all the elements of culture of the most highly civilized communities, and of playing an honourable part in the complex life of such a community. They delight in telling us how the native children in this or that missionary school excel their white fellows in learning the A B C, or even in acquiring the Three R's. Especially they avoid the direct issue by demonstrating at length the obvious truth that race and nationality are not coincident. This is merely a red herring drawn across the track, to put us off the scent. The " race-slumpers " have shown, it must be admitted, that the facile generalizations of many historians upon race and national character have been of the most flimsy nature, often erroneous and sometimes absurd. We must recognize with them that these flimsy assumptions have worked harm ; and we must agree with them in condemning in the most outspoken way the evil work of the more extreme race dogmatists.[1]

But when Mr. Oakesmith concludes that the practical value of " race " is purely subjective ; that " race " is merely an emotion, like that of the soldier who is proud of his regiment's history ; when the " race-slumpers " assert or imply, as they do, that all men are born with the same mental endowments, that all human stocks are of equal value, and that the anthropologic composition of a people

---

[1] Oakesmith (p. 58) says of Chamberlain's work : " It is false in its theories ; ludicrously inaccurate in its assertions ; pompous and extravagant in its style ; insolent to its critics and opponents." With these strictures I entirely agree.

is of no influence upon the course of its history, then we must part company from them. These writers have shown that the training of the pure historian does not qualify him to propound sweeping generalizations about racial qualities ; and that, when he undertakes to do so, in entire ignorance of the findings of anthropology and equipped only with the fallacious psychology which is embodied in common speech, he cannot hope to arrive at the truth. They have shown that the historian, if he would rightly interpret or explain the course of the history of peoples, rather than be content merely to describe it, must go to school with the anthropologists, must take account of all their findings, and must wait patiently until we shall have accumulated more data and a surer insight into that obscurest and most difficult of all problems with which science is concerned—the mental constitution of man and its subtle variations.

In all this question of race and nationality we need, in short, to make a new start. Instead of throwing ourselves passionately into one or other of the opposed camps, the camp of the race-dogmatists or that of the race-slumpers, we must examine the evidence afresh with strict impartiality, unmoved by national prejudice or by humanitarian sentiment. Especially we must disentangle and clearly distinguish between national character and racial or ethnic qualities. For the confusion of these conceptions has been the root of most of the trouble. National character, as I have

53

taken some pains to show,[1] is not the mere sum or average of individual characters or qualities. But that is not to say that individual qualities play no part in shaping national character. Both parties have made the mistake of regarding national character as the sum or average of individual qualities ; the race-dogmatists assuming that the nation in all its doings always expresses certain individual qualities, which they assume to be common to all members of the nation ; the race-slumpers pointing out in return that, at different periods of its history, a nation exhibits itself in very different characters ; for example, they point out that the Jews were at one time an agricultural and warlike people, but that in modern times they have seemed very averse from both agriculture and war ; and they deduce from such facts the conclusion that the qualities of any population are completely fluid and indefinite.

It will, I think, help us to define our problem more exactly, if we state it concretely in the following way.[2] Let us imagine that in some one of the great well-defined nations—say the British—every infant, throughout a period of fifty years, could be exchanged without the knowledge of its

[1] " The Group Mind. A Sketch of the Principles of Collective Psychology with Some Attempt to Apply Them to the Interpretation of National Life and Character." London, 1920.

[2] As I did some twelve years ago in my " Introduction to Social Psychology," p. 330, fifteenth edition. London, 1920.

parents for an infant of another people. If this were done, at the close of the period of fifty years the anthropologic constitution of the nation would have been completely changed or exchanged. Would that affect the future course of its national life ? If so, in what manner and degree ? If we suppose the exchange to have been made with some other nation of similar composition and level of culture, the race-slumpers—Messrs. Finot, Oakesmith, Robertson—would confidently reply : " No, it would make no difference." Would they give the same reply if the exchange were made with some remoter people, say the Japanese, or Armenians, or Italians , or with a still remoter people, say the Hottentots or the Bushmen of southern Africa, or the Malays of the Far East ? Their principles logically would compel them to give the same reply ; but I fancy that, when confronted with the issue in this concrete form, the most extreme of them would hesitate to do so. They would probably put us off with some reference to physical incompatibility of climate, and so forth. For these writers do not and cannot deny important physical peculiarities of race ; their negation applies only to differences of mental endowment, in respect of which the establishment of the facts is so much more difficult.

Let us see, then, what evidence we have bearing on this great question of differences of innate mental endowment. And we will begin with the problem of intellectual endowment, or innate capacity for the development of intellect or intelli-

55

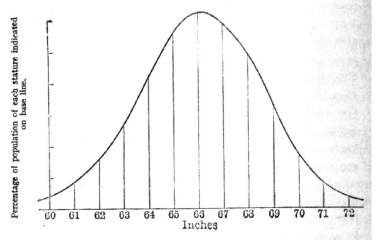

FIGURE I

A normal curve of distribution of stature in a population, the average stature of which is 66 inches.

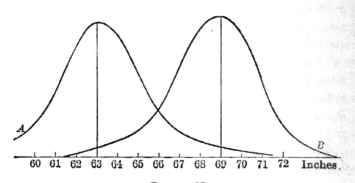

FIGURE II

The overlapping curves of distribution of stature in two homogeneous populations of which one (A) has the average stature of 63 inches, the other (B) 69 inches.

gence. For, though the moral factors may be more important, intelligence is a valuable quality and not to be despised; and it is more easily measurable than the moral qualities.

Let us notice, first, that in Anthropology we have to deal with human beings in mass, and have to treat our facts by statistical methods, as far as possible. Therefore the pointing to individual cases of the presence of well-marked qualities, even if such cases be numerous, is out of order, and merely confuses the issue. Consider this for a moment in relation to a simply measured physical quality, say stature. When the anthropologist asserts that one population, A, is shorter than another, B, he is speaking of averages; he does not mean to deny that tall men may be found in A and short men in B; and to point to even extreme instances of such aberration from the average does not invalidate his generalization. If the two populations contrasted are fairly homogeneous, the statures of each may be represented roughly by a curve, the abscissæ of which represent the various heights, each ordinate the percentage of the population which has the height marked on the horizontal line. These are the normal curves of distribution. Or, if one population is mixed or formed by the intermarriage of two stocks of unequal stature, it may show a double peak.[1] In either case the average stature is a

[1] Such a double-peaked curve would result if the two populations represented by the curves A and B of Fig. II were mixed and the measurements of stature of a large

significant figure ; and the generalization remains valid, even though you point to very tall men among A and to short men among B. In considering mental qualities, we must keep this way of viewing the facts constantly in mind, and must avoid the fallacy of seeking to upset generalizations by pointing to exceptional instances.

The example of stature is instructive by analogy in another way. When two populations are found to differ in average stature, we are not justified in assuming forthwith that this difference expresses a difference of innate constitution. We must inquire first into the conditions under which the two populations live. If A lives in an infertile area, under conditions of hardship and poor nutrition, its lower stature may be due to this fact. For there are clear instances in which low stature of a whole population may be traced to such causes. Only if the conditions are favourable to the full development of stature in both groups does difference of the average stature imply difference of innate constitution. But, when such influences have been taken into account and allowed for, it appears clearly that the stature of men, or the extent of their growth in stature, is, even under the most favourable conditions, determined and limited by

sample of the mixed population were plotted on a single curve. Such double-peaked curves of physical qualities have been found, *e.g.*, the curve of distribution of the cephalic index among the Greeks of Asia Minor (Ripley, " Races of Europe," p. 116).

innate constitution. By taking thought a boy may add a little to his stature, but the amount he may so add is strictly limited. Further, stature is hereditary. Here again the statement is true statistically ; and the statistical-generalization is not invalidated by instances of tall sons born of short parents. What we mean by the statement is that, on the average, the sons of short forefathers will be, under equally good conditions, shorter than the sons of tall forefathers. Now, apply these ways of thinking to mental qualities, and we shall find evidence that intellectual stature and intellectual growth are subject to generalizations very similar to those which are found to hold good for physical stature and physical growth. This is an all-important thesis, fundamental to our whole problem.

The " race-slumpers," in their denial, both explicit and implied, of all significant differences between one man and another as regards mental qualities, are the champions of common sense and the view of the plain man—views in which the plain man has been supported by both law and medicine until very recent years. For the plain man, and law and medicine also, accepted the traditional assumption that our mental powers are the expression of a supernatural principle, the soul, miraculously implanted in each one of us at birth ; and, while they recognized great differences of bodily endowment, they ignored comparable differences of mental endowment, with certain exceptions. The man of genius on the one hand, the idiot and the madman on the other hand, were mysterious exceptions; but, apart from these exceptions, all men were born equal, and all differences of attainment were attributed to differences of opportunity and education; all men had equal powers and equal responsibilities, and must be treated as strictly alike, unless their departure from the average was so extreme that they might claim to be men of genius, madmen, or idiots. Of such cases common sense, the law, and medicine washed their hands, disclaiming all responsibility—for they did not fit into the theory; the genius was allowed to go his own way, the madmen and idiots were handed over to special institutions and there secluded.

Very recently a step forward has been made in this connection. Medical men have recognized that idiots, the poor creatures whose defect of intellect is so great as to be obvious, as it were, to the naked eye, are not sharply marked off as a class from their fellow-men. They have sought and found many transitional forms which connect the idiot with the normal or average man; and they have devised appropriate terms by which to denote those who approximate in various degrees to the conditions of the idiot. The law has come to their help and has constituted a class of "mental defectives," persons whose intellectual capacities are so poor that they cannot be regarded as fully responsible, but who must, for their own sakes, be put into special schools and institutions; because they cannot profit by the educational processes provided for the normal child, cannot compete on even terms with the normal man. In these schools and institutions they have been carefully studied, and the following facts fully established. Many of them differ greatly. from the idiot (who generally has defects of brain and body obvious to the eye) in that to the untrained observer they appear to be normal persons ; and their brains and physical development, even to the skilled observer, present no marked peculiarities. Nevertheless, do what you will for these people, lavish upon them, from their earliest infancy, all the skill and care of specialists in medicine and education, and you cannot make them into normal adults, fully responsible persons, capable of holding their own in the world. The best of them, after being carefully trained and taught some simple trade, can go out into the world and, under favourable conditions, can earn a living, marry and produce children, and lead more or less useful respectable lives. Others (and there are all grades and no sharp divisions) cannot be brought to this level ; if they are sent out into the world to lead the normal life, they fail and become paupers, tramps, or hoboes ; or they appear again and again in the police courts for trivial offences. Others are so obviously defective that they cannot be allowed to attempt to lead the normal life ; and they are kept, much to their own benefit, in the appropriate institutions, harmless and happy, and often, in a limited way, useful. These people illustrate the truth of what I said in my first chapter of the increasing demands of civilization upon the qualities of its bearers. In earlier times and in simpler communities such people undoubtedly existed or exist ; but under those simpler conditions their defects would not disqualify them for the common life. In a simple rural community they may rub along fairly well. The mental defect of these persons, their defect of intelligence, is, then, not due to lack of education or opportunity ; it is an inborn constitutional defect.

A second great fact has been established by the modern study of these mental defectives—namely, that their defect is not only inborn, or innate ; it is also hereditary. In most cases it is inherited from similar parents or grandparents ; and, if they produce children, it is likely to be transmitted to some or all of them. We do not yet fully understand the laws of its transmission ; but one fact seems to be fully established : if two such defectives marry and produce children, all those children will also be " mental defectives."

In recent years an immense amount of study has been devoted to these cases by highly competent workers.[1] The facts as stated are established. No recitation of instances of boys who have risen to eminence from the gutter can shake them. May we suppose, then, that these mental defectives form a class sharply marked off from

[1] See Doctor H. H. Goddard's " Human Efficiency and Levels of Intelligence," and his " Psychology of the Normal and Abnormal." Princeton, 1920.

normal persons, as it used to be assumed that the idiots formed a class sharply marked off ? Or is it possible that intelligence or intellectual stature closely resembles physical stature in respect of its distribution through the population ? Evidence is fast accumulating to show that this view is true. An important step in mental anthropology has recently been made. The method of intelligence-tests (or mental testing) has been devised, and in the American army and elsewhere has been assiduously applied. The methods have been proved on a scale which shows that the results achieved are " statistically " valid, though errors may and do occur in individual cases. Popular opinion of " mental testing " is naturally divided : those of us who did well when tested naturally think it a good system ; those of us who did badly incline to the opinion that it is an absurd academic fad. But the evidence that its results are statistically valid is overwhelming.

I put before you a sample of the results obtained in the testing of a large batch (many thousands) of American recruits from a given area. This particular sample (which I owe to the kindness of one of my pupils, Mr. N. D. Hirsch, who took part in the conduct of the testing) is especially interesting, because it includes both white and coloured recruits, and because these were drawn from an area in which facilities for schooling were relatively poor, so that many of these recruits had enjoyed very little schooling or none at all. The Table I shows

TABLE I

	A	B	C+	C	C−	D	D−	E
W. L. . .	2·6	6	12	26	23	28	0	0
W. I. . .	·2	1·4	3·3	14	19	37	22	2
C. L. . .	1·0	1·4	3 1	9	19	39	26	0
C. I. . .	·5	·3	·5	3·2	8	33	46	7

the recruits arranged in four classes : white literates (W. L.), white illiterates (W. I.), coloured literates (C. L.), and coloured illiterates (C. I.). The individuals of each of these classes are distributed in percentages under eight letters, in the order of decreasing intelligence.

There are many interesting features about this table. We see that each class taken by itself gives approximately an asymmetrical curve[1] of distribution of intelligence. The curves for the white illiterates and the coloured literates run pretty closely together, indicating that these two classes show approximately the same degree of intelligence " statistically " ; while the white literates' curve shows considerable shift to the left, and that of the coloured illiterates a shift to the right.

You may be disposed at first sight to attribute the differences of intelligence disclosed to differences of degree of education, of schooling ; but

[1] The reader can easily picture for himself the curve of distribution implied by the figures for each of the four classes.

64

reflection shows that the assumption will not fit the facts.

First, the tests were deliberately designed in order to give no advantage to the more educated man as such. But, you may say, his education has made him more intelligent. Well, perhaps it has in some degree. But if education is the source of the difference between the white literates and the white illiterates, and between the coloured literates and the coloured illiterates—what has made the difference between white and coloured ? Again, what makes the difference between the groups A to E in each class ? They must be in the main native differences. A men occur in all classes. Further evidence of this may be seen in the nature of the curves. Each taken alone is asymmetrical. If we amalgamate the two curves for whites and the two curves for coloureds, we get curves nearer a normal curve of distribution. But both curves will still show a too abrupt descent on the right. This is partly accounted for if we remember that a certain number of young men were rejected at sight as obviously unfit to serve, including all the declared mental defectives. The addition of them would bring both curves nearer to the form of a normal symmetrical curve of distribution. Further, when a large group of college students were tested (three thousand men, all of whom had enjoyed the advantages of full school and some college education) they were found to spread out in a similar wide curve of widely different grades ; the

5   65

curve is not so wide as the curve representing all the whites of Table I, because the lower grades (D and E) are missing altogether. It resembles closely the curve for the white literates. Here the educational factor has been practically the same for all, yet the degrees of intellectual capacity as revealed by the tests are widely spread.

All these facts point to the one conclusion, namely, that innate capacity for intellectual growth is the predominant factor in determining the distribution of intelligence in adults, and that the amount and kind of education is a factor of subordinate importance.

The superiority of the white literates to the white illiterates is due, then, not wholly or mainly to their schooling, but rather to an inborn greater capacity for intellectual growth. Spontaneous selection has been at work in this region, where schooling is difficult to obtain ; and, on the whole, those boys most fitted by nature to profit by schooling have obtained it. It must be noted that the class of illiterates includes many boys who attended school for a few years only and then dropped out. Does not common experience teach us that, where schooling is difficult to obtain, the brighter boys who find themselves making good progress in school are those who are most likely to continue at school ? And is it not probable that the brighter boys and the sons of the more intelligent parents are more likely to enter school than the dullards and the sons of unintelligent parents ?

Another point of interest is suggested by Table II, expressed in " mental age."[1] The difference

TABLE II

	MENTAL AGE.	DIFFERENCE.
W. L.	14·5 ⎫	
W. I.	12·2 ⎬	2·3
C. L.	12·1 ⎫	
C. I.	10·8 ⎬	1·5

between literates and illiterates is due partly to innate differences, partly to education; but the difference is much greater in whites than in coloureds. If we assume that the attraction of the schools works selectively in equal degree on whites and coloureds, and this seems a fair assumption, then it follows that the higher the level of innate capacity, the more is it improved by education.

Finally, when all the white recruits of the whole army are thrown into a single table, they give a curve conforming very closely to a normal curve of distribution.[2]

Such findings require confirmation by the more thorough testing of practical life, and they have had such thorough confirmation. For example, of a large group of college students who, after

[1] A conventional scale in which the position of a very intelligent adult is expressed by the figure 20.
[2] See p. 57.

being tested, entered an officers' training-school, many were eventually rejected because they proved unfit to be officers. Of those who scored A or B in the tests at entry, eight-ninths passed through the school successfully; of those who scored C— or D, seven-eighths failed; of those who scored C, 50 per cent. failed. Further, it was found that men who scored below C generally proved inadequate to the duties of a non-commissioned officer.

The official report, after carefully weighing all the evidence, states: "These examinations were intended, and are now definitely known, to measure native intellectual ability; they are to some extent influenced by educational acquirement, but in the main the soldier's inborn intelligence and not the accidents of environment determines his mental rating."[1]

[1] "Army Mental Tests" by P. S. Yoakum and R. M. Yerkes, 1920, p. 17. Professor S. M. Terman (who has had large experience in the application of mental tests to children) writes: "We are beginning to learn that all of these measures combined are powerless to reduce greatly the number of over-age children in the grades. Notwithstanding the persistent campaign which has been waged against the evils of retardation for the last dozen years, the number of retardates remains to-day much the same as it was when the campaign began. . . . The facts . . . point fairly definitely to the conclusion that the differences which have been found to exist among children in physical traits are paralleled by equal differences in mental traits, particularly intelligence. It will be shown that these innate differences in intelligence are chiefly responsible for the problem of the school laggard." ("The Intelligence of School Children," p. 24.)

CHAPTER III

THE evidence cited in the foregoing chapter shows that in the population of America innate intellectual capacity (or the capacity to develop intelligence) is continuously distributed, in much the same fashion as a physical quality such as stature. It is true that we cannot exactly define this vague thing which we measure and call " intellectual capacity." Is it a simple unitary factor which may be a Mendelian unit ? Some psychologists, using a most ingenious statistical method (the method of correlation and the hierarchy), have argued that these various levels of intellectual capacity depend on the possession of more or less of such a single common factor which they call general intelligence or the " G factor " ; and they have proposed to call it " intellective energy."[1] You may object that this a vague notion, and may ask—What exactly is this intellective energy ? It is fair to reply that it is something which we can measure and recognize, though we cannot describe

---

[1] *Cf.* especially papers by Professor C. Spearman, Mr. C. Burt, and others in the *British Journal of Psychology*, and Doctor Maxwell Garnett's "Education and World-Citizenship." London, 1921.

it or adequately conceive it ; and that in this respect it is just like electricity or other physical energies which the engineer measures and controls but cannot fully understand or adequately describe. But, even if this is a mistaken view, and if the level of intellectual capacity is a resultant of many factors, that does not invalidate the conception for anthropological purposes. Physical stature (or the capacity to attain a certain stature) is a resultant of many factors (lengths of many bones), yet it is an inborn or innate quality ; though affected by environment, yet it is determined by heredity ; it is inborn in various degrees in individuals and in races, some having more and others less of it ; and the same is true of intellectual capacity.

This conclusion is distasteful ; for it sets a limit to the power of education. It may seem likely to discourage the enthusiasts of education ; but it should not do that. Even though the effects of education are limited by Nature, it is of the highest importance that we make the most and the best of the human material which she supplies. Those who resent this limitation of the power of education are very apt to struggle against the conclusion by an argument of this kind. They describe instances of boys, taken from a deplorable environment and from undesirable parents, who, having been put under good conditions and given good education, have become useful or even distinguished citizens. But even a large number of such cases can do nothing to invalidate our conclusion. They may be set off completely by citing cases of the opposite type, cases of boys who, though denied every opportunity for schooling, nevertheless have attained to the very highest levels of distinction—boys like Abraham Lincoln or George Stephenson, the creator of the English railways.

Let us look now a little more closely at the racial distribution of intellectual capacity. Unfortunately, facts are few, and, though I would rather choose for discussion any other race than the Negro, they alone of the coloured peoples have been studied in a way which makes possible a comparison with the white population.

TÁBLE III.

	A	B	C+	C	C—	D	D—	E
Whites . .	2·0	4·8	9·7	20	22	30	8	2
Coloureds .	·8	1·0	1·9	6	15	37	30	7
Officers . .	55·0	29·0	12·0	4	0	0	0	0

That races are endowed in different degrees with innate intellectual capacity is implied by the difference between the curves for whites and coloureds (Table III). We have seen that the curve for the coloured literates almost coincides with that for the white illiterates. We have seen that the difference of level between the white literates and illiterates is determined in part by education, in part by natural endowment. Note, then, that

71

whichever factor is predominant, or if either alone is responsible, the racial difference of native endowment stands out clearly.

Now, the coloured men of America are largely, I suppose, of mixed white and Negro descent. It may be suggested that the native inferiority of the coloured in respect of this quality (intelligence) is an evil effect of the cross-breeding of these two widely dissimilar races. That is a possibility. But facts are strongly against it. First, the coloured men of the Northern States showed distinct superiority to those of the South, in respect of their performance in the army intelligence-tests. Have they not a larger proportion of white blood ? I do not know, but I suspect it.

Secondly, we have the fact that some of the leaders of the coloured people deliberately advocate the improvement of the coloured people by further miscegenation. A fact not conclusive, but a significant admission.

Thirdly, we have the allegation, frequently made, that every coloured man who has risen to high distinction has been of mixed blood. It is perhaps difficult to prove the rule ; but it is difficult to find exceptions.[1]

[1] The late Professor N. S. Shaler was a close student of the coloured people and was affectionately disposed toward them. In his book " The Neighbour " (Boston, 1904), which bears on every page the marks of the spirit of justice and benevolence, he states : " Almost all the Negroes of this country who have shown marked capacity of any kind have had an evident mixture of white blood " (p. 163). He mentions a single exception.

Fourthly, we have a few studies which suggest that, when two races of different intellectual capacity are crossed, the offspring are (statistically) intermediate, and that they approximate to the superior race according to the proportion of their blood derived from it.

As regards the Negro race, I know of no such study ; probably the descent of the coloured people cannot be traced with sufficient accuracy for this purpose.[1]

But we have two recent studies of Indians and cross-breeds of white and Indian blood, made quite independently by different observers and by different methods in different places. The Indians studied were all literates, pupils in Indian schools and colleges. The results of the two investigations agree. One observer[2] concludes that the Indians of mixed

[1] Professor R. S. Woodworth, in an article on the " Comparative Psychology of Races " (*Psychological Bulletin*, Vol. XIII, 1916), summarizes the findings of three observers, all of whom, applying " intelligence-tests " to white and coloured children, found the intellectual capacity of the coloureds to be (statistically) inferior to that of the whites. One of them (Ferguson) divided the coloured children into four groups according to the depths of colouration, and, accepting shade of colour as an indication of the proportion of white blood, concluded, that " in the more intellectual tests, success increased with the proportion of white blood." Shaler wrote : " It is a common opinion held by the blacks as well as the whites that an infusion of white blood increases the intelligence of the Negro, while at the same time lowering his moral qualities." *Ibid* , p. 162

[2] Mr. T. R. Garth (University of Texas).

blood are superior in intellectual capacity to the full-blooded Indians by one full year of mental age. The other (Professor Hunter, University of Kansas) compared white children with Indians of full blood, and with those of one-quarter, one-half, and three-quarters of white blood ; he shows that there is a large difference in intellectual capacity between the white and the Indian, and that the cross-bred approximate to the white level in proportion to their share of white blood ; and, after carefully considering all the possibilities, cautiously concludes that the difference is probably due to race.[1]

It seems highly probable, then, that the same rule holds good for the mulatto, and that, if pure Negroes were compared with whites, the difference of intellectual capacity would be considerably greater than that actually found between whites and coloureds.[2]

[1] Summaries of the work of Mr. Garth and Mr. Hunter appear in the reports of the meeting of the American Psychological Association at Chicago, December, 1920 (*Psychological Bulletin*, 1921).

[2] In the *Journal of Applied Psychology* for 1919 Messrs. S. L. Pressey and G. F. Teter report " A Comparison of Coloured and White Children by Means of a Group-Scale of Intelligence." They examined 187 coloured and 2,800 white children of the same ages and drawn from the schools of the same area. They conclude : " The coloured children of a given age average at about the average for white children (in the same city) two years younger " ; and they add : " Analysis by test shows the coloured children to average below white children of the same age on all the tests." This difference between white and coloured children is the more significant, if we take into account the

NATIONAL WELFARE AND NATIONAL DECAY

This conclusion is in harmony with the indications afforded by the whole history of the Negro race—not only in Africa and America, but in Oceania and especially in such regions as Haiti and Liberia. It is not in the least invalidated by the statistics we so often see, showing the progress of the coloured people since emancipation, and by the acknowledged fact that some men of colour have shown themselves to be truly great men.[1]

Now let us turn to a second question. These differences of intellectual capacity are inborn; but are they hereditary? We have already noted

view which is widely held and which is probably true of many if not of all cases, namely, that inequality of adult intelligence is due, not so much to more rapid development of the more intelligent throughout childhood, but rather to an earlier arrest of development in the less intelligent.

[1] Shaler, who made a lifelong study of the Negroes and who wrote with warm appreciation of their many fine qualities, recorded, nevertheless, the following judgment. " All the facts we have point to the same unhappy conclusion, that the Negro considered as a species is, by nature, incapable of creating or maintaining societies of an order above barbarism, and that, so far as we can discern, this feature of his nature, depending, as it does, on the lack of certain qualities of mind, is irremediable " (" The Neighbour," p. 139). Again he wrote : " Unlike the most of the people who come to us from Europe, his race [the Negro] is not provided with the motives that lead to safety. His elevation and maintenance, so far as we can see, for all time absolutely depend upon the help he is to receive from the state-building race " (*op. cit.*, p. 172). It is thus apparent that the results of the recent application of the exacter methods of mental measurement bear out the opinion of impartial judges based upon long and careful observation of the less exact kind.

certain facts which imply the positive answer. If the differences are racial, they are hereditary in the race. But within the same race, or in a population blended from many closely allied stocks, such as the English or the white Americans, are they hereditary ?

Well, we have seen that the lower levels, the levels of the mental defectives, are hereditary. Further, medical men have shown certain other forms of " mental defect " to be hereditary, e.g., certain forms of insanity, or rather the predisposition to these, also the predisposition to epilepsy and the neuroses.

At the other end, the upper end of the scale, the studies of Galton[1] and his disciples have shown good ground for believing that exceptionally high intellectual capacity is hereditary. Standing alone, Galton's reasoning is perhaps inconclusive ; and many have sought to escape his conclusions by attributing the achievements of the sons and grandsons of great men to their superior opportunities. But, when taken with the rest of the evidence, Galton's conclusions seem to me to be in the main incontestable, for they are in line with and harmonize with all the rest.

If, then, the degrees of intellectual capacity at the extremes of the scale are hereditary, it seems highly probable that the same is true of the intermediate part of the scale. But have we any direct evidence of this ? Is there any evidence that the

[1] " Hereditary Genius."

intellectual capacity of the ordinary plain citizen
is determined largely by heredity ? Common observation seems to point that way, but it is inconclusive
And we have hitherto only the beginnings of a
direct attack on this problem. Professor K. Pearson[1]
has produced evidence that mental qualities are
transmissible in exactly the same degree as physical
qualities. He is a great statistician, but the mental
qualities he dealt with are vague ill-defined conceptions, and his conclusions are perhaps open to
criticism on that ground. Some years before the
war one of my pupils at Oxford made a direct attack
on the problem, and the results are significant, though
on a small scale. At Oxford are gathered as teachers
many men from the whole British Empire, highly
selected in virtue of intellectual distinction. Now
it so happens that in a certain private school in
Oxford a majority of the boys are sons of these men.
We therefore set out to compare the intellectual
capacity of the boys of this school with that of boys
of a primary school. This primary school was an
exceptionally good school of its kind, the teaching
being in many respects better than in the other—
the private school ; the boys were from good homes,
sons of good plain citizens—shopkeepers and skilled
artisans, and so forth—and there was no question
of their development having been retarded by
physical privations.

Without going into detail, I may say summarily
that the result was to show a very marked superiority

[1] " Biometrika," Vol. III.

of the boys of the school frequented by the intellectual class.[1] The result is all the more striking, if you reflect on the following facts : First, every boy has two parents and inherits his qualities from both. Secondly, it has not been shown that university dons prefer clever wives, or that they are particularly clever in choosing clever wives. There is room for difference of opinion. It remains, then, highly probable that, if the wives of these men were all as superior in respect in intellect as their husbands, the superiority of their sons to the boys of the other group would have been still more marked.

The result suggests a question of very great interest. Does the social stratification of society correspond to, is it correlated with, a stratification of intellectual capacity ? The positive answer has been widely assumed on general grounds of probability by those who have studied heredity.

[1] Mr. H. B. English, who conducted this research, has reported it in the *Yale Psychological Studies* for 1917 : " Mental Capacity of School Children Correlated with Social Status." Mr. English concludes : " Although the groups are small, they are exceedingly homogeneous and thoroughly representative of the children in two social or economic strata. The writer does not hesitate, therefore, to predicate these results for the children of the entire classes represented or to conclude that the children of the professional class exhibit between 12 and 14 years of age a very marked superiority in intelligence." " Although he is not prepared to say, and does not in fact believe, that environment has had nothing to do with the superiority of one group over the other, he is convinced that *the heredi-tary factor* plays an altogether predominant part."— *Cf.* footnote, p. 189.

Others ridicule the idea and produce, as usual, their instances which do not conform to any such general rule. The result of the research just now mentioned supports the positive answer.

But the question is extremely important, and I cite therefore the results of another direct attack on the problem.[1] Miss A. H. Arlitt (of Bryn Mawr College) tested 342 children from the primary grades of schools of one district. Of these, 191 were of American-born white parents, 80 were born of Italian immigrants, 71 were coloured. They all spoke English without difficulty. The Americans were divided, according to the social status of their parents, into five groups, corresponding to those defined by Professor Taussig: (1) professional; (2) semi-professional and higher business; (3) skilled labour; (4) semi-skilled labour; and (5) unskilled labour. Groups (4) and (5) were amalgamated.

The results show very marked differences between the groups. They give four dissimilar curves of distribution. The medians (I.Q.) of the four groups were (1) 125, (2) 118, (3) 107, (4) 92. I.Q. stands for " intelligence quotient," and is commonly used

---

[1] I may cite also similar results obtained by another of my pupils at Oxford, Mr. Cyril Burt, who concludes his article as follows : " For all these reasons we may conclude that the superior proficiency at intelligence-tests on the part of the boys of superior parentage was inborn. And thus we seem to have proved marked inheritability in the case of a mental character of the highest ' civic worth.' " " Experimental Tests of General Intelligence," *British Journal of Psychology*, Vol. III, 1909.

as a convenient abbreviation for "intellectual capacity as revealed by mental testing." The "median" is considered to be a rather more satisfactory figure than "the average" for the comparison of one group with another ; it is commonly not widely different from "the average." The following table expresses the grades of intelligence attributed to the various groups on the basis of the testing

TABLE IV

Americans of social status (1)			.	.	.	I. Q.	=	125
,,	,, ,,	,, (2)	.	.	.	I. Q.	=	118
,,	,, ,,	,, (3)	.	.	.	I. Q.	=	107
,,	,, ,,	,, (4)	.	.	.	I. Q.	=	92
Italians						I. Q.	=	84 [1]
Coloured						I. Q.	=	83
All Americans grouped together .			.	.		I. Q.	=	106

---

[1] If this figure should be confirmed by further research, it would, of course, not justify us in drawing any inference about the population of Italy as a whole, nor even about that of Southern Italy, from which region most of these immigrants have probably come. The recent Italian immigrants are probably not a fair sample of the population of Italy. I have omitted the decimal figures from Miss Arlitt's figures. I am much indebted to her for sending me details of her observations. Her full paper has not yet been published (summary in *Psychological Bulletin*, February, 1921).

It is noteworthy that Professor Terman, a high authority, has found similar indications in working with the children of Italian and Spanish and Portuguese immigrants. In his book ("Intelligence of School Children," New York, 1919, p. 56) he gives the following figures for the I.Q., or measure of relative intelligence of the following classes of children drawn from the same schools :

A third research of a similar kind points to the same conclusion.[1] Tests were made of 548 children from the schools of one city. The children were arranged in four groups according to the occupation of their father, namely professional, executive, artisan, labour. The results are stated in terms of the percentage of children of each group who scored a mark higher than the median mark for the whole number of 548 children, and are as follows :—Professional group, 85 per cent. ; executive group, 68 per cent. ; artisan group, 41 per cent. ; labour group, 39 per cent.[2]

Spanish	78
Portuguese	84
Italian	84
North European	105
American	106

[1] S. L. Pressey and R. Ralston, *Journal of Applied Psychology*, Vol. III, 1919 : " The Relation of General Intelligence of School Children to Occupation of the Father."

[2] Professor Terman, reporting on the results of tests applied to a large number of American school children, states : " Intelligence of 110 to 120 I.Q. [this range is defined as ' superior intelligence,' the bulk of the children, about 60 per cent , ranging from 90 to 110 I.Q.] is approximately five times as common among children of superior social status as among children of inferior social status, the proportion among the former being about 24 per cent. of all and among the latter only 5 per cent. of all. The group [i e , the group of ' superior intelligence '] is made up largely of children of the fairly successful mercantile or professional classes." He defines as of " very superior intelligence " those children who scored in the tests more than 120 marks. " Children of this group are . . . unusually superior. Not more than 3 out of 100 (i.e., of all

6

We have, then, pretty good evidence that capacity for intellectual growth is inborn in different degrees, that it is hereditary, and also that it is closely correlated with social status.[1] Further, we have good evidence that different races possess it in widely different degrees ; that races differ in intellectual stature, just as they differ in physical stature.

We have considered so far only one human quality, intellectual capacity. This is very important. But other qualities also are important. We know how a man or a boy of normal, or superior, intellectual capacity may fail to make good for lack of moral qualities. We know that the moral qualities show a considerable independence of intellectual

tested) go as high as 125 I.Q., and only about 1 out of 100 as high as 130. In the schools of a city of average population only about 1 child in 250 or 300 tests as high as 140 I.Q. In a series of 476 unselected children there was not a single one reaching 120 whose social class was described as ' below average.' Of the children of superior social status, about 10 per cent. reached 120 or better. The 120–140 group (i.e., of very superior intelligence) is made up almost entirely of children whose parents belong to the professional or very successful business classes. The child of a skilled labourer belongs here occasionally, the child of a common labourer very rarely indeed. At least this is true in the smaller cities of California among populations made up of native-born Americans." (" The Measurement of Intelligence," p. 95, New York, 1916.)

[1] It seems highly probable that degrees of intelligence are not merely correlated with degrees of social status, but that intelligence is related to social status as ground to consequent or cause to effect. For yet another piece of evidence supporting this all-important conclusion, see p. 156.

capacity. In regard to them the same questions arise. Are they inborn in various degrees ? Are they hereditary ? Are they distributed in different degrees and combinations in races and in the strata of the population of such a country as America ?

These questions are even more difficult, and more apt to provoke acute differences of opinion, than the similar questions regarding intellectual capacity. Experimental psychology has hardly begun to contemplate these problems ; we have to glean our evidence from other sources. One small piece obtained by the experimental method seems worth citing as a suggestion. Mr. K. T. Waugh applied a number of tests to students in four colleges of British India (Lucknow), one Chinese college, and some American colleges. The tests were largely concerned with memory, and were not well suited to test intellectual capacity. They revealed only slight differences, which were slightly in favour of the Indian students—except in one quality, namely, power of concentrating the attention.[1] In this the Chinese exactly equalled the Americans ; the Indians fell decidedly short of them. The facts that in other tests the Indians equalled or excelled

[1] Mr. Waugh's report was made to the meeting of the American Psychological Association at Chicago, December, 1920 ("Comparison of Oriental and American Student Intelligence "). The functions tested were (1) concentration of attention, (2) speed of learning, (3) association-time, (4) immediate memory, (5) deferred memory, (6) range of information His results are embodied in the following table :

the Americans, and that in two tests, which measure the power of concentration of attention, the Chinese equalled, while the Indians fell far short of the Americans—these facts inspire confidence in the objectivity of this result. They go far to show that the differences found are not due to racial bias in favour of his own race on the part of the observer, or to conditions of experimenting unduly favourable to the American students. This result seems to me extraordinarily interesting and suggestive. For what is this power of concentrating attention? It is essentially will-power. I need only refer to what William James wrote of this.[1] Now the

Where retentiveness is equal but speed of learning unequal, and power of concentration correlated with superior

TEST	SCORES		
	AMERICAN.	CHINESE	INDIAN
1	75	75	62
2	66	62	45
3	46	38	58
4	58	—	54
5	80	—	88
6	23	15	24

speed of learning, we may safely attribute the superiority in speed to superiority of concentration.

[1] " Effort of attention is thus the essential phenomenon of will " (" Principles of Psychology," Vol. II, p. 562). Compare also the discussion and similar conclusion on this topic in Doctor Maxwell Garnett's " Education and World-Citizenship."

more or less orderly and successful government of the 300,000,000 of India by a mere handful of British men, during more than a century, is one of the most remarkable facts in the history of the world. It is a marvellous achievement. And Englishmen have marvelled over it. And, when they have sought to explain how it has been possible, they have always come to the same conclusion. They have recognized that the natives of India, or very many of them, have much intellectual capacity ; that they are clever, quick, versatile, retentive ; that some of them have brilliant intellects. But such observers have frequently expressed the opinion that, as compared with their British rulers, the natives of India are relatively defective in character or will-power ; and they have found the explanation of British ascendancy in this fact. Now, at the very first attempt to apply exact methods in the comparative study of Indians, this opinion finds confirmation. If this conclusion is really well-founded, as it seems to be, might we not infer from. it that, if the qualities of Indians and British had been reversed in this single respect—if the Indians were as innately superior in will-power as they seem to be inferior—then, not improbably, a few Indians would at the present time be ruling over and administering the affairs of all Europe and perhaps of all America as well ? It is a strange reflection. It is not utterly fantastic and absurd. It may at least serve to suggest how profoundly peculiarities of moral constitution may affect the destinies of peoples.

NATIONAL WELFARE AND NATIONAL DECAY

In this connexion it should be remembered that the quelling of the Indian Mutiny was, before all things, a triumph of will-power. If even a few of the British leaders, if Havelock, John Nicholson, and Baird Smith, and one or two others had failed, ever so little, in the supreme tests of will-power from which they came out triumphant, the British would have been swept from the country, and British rule in India would have been brought to an end about the year 1857.

CHAPTER IV

THE moral factors of human nature are very complex. Let us turn to the field of art, and see whether we cannot find in the arts of Europe the expression of racial peculiarities of moral constitution. The problem of racial manifestations in Europe would be simpler if we could assume, as has sometimes been done, that the population of Europe, or of western Europe, represents in the main two distinct races, the so-called Latin and Teutonic races. But anthropologists are pretty well agreed that it is derived in the main from three distinct races, which, although much mixed and partially blended in all countries, are spread out in three great east-to-west bands; the tall fair Nordic race in the North; the short dark longheaded Mediterranean race in the South; the darkish round-headed Alpine race in between; that is to say, the blood of each of these races predominates in these three zones respectively. In spite of this complication, we may contrast the art of the South with that of the North, and inquire how far any constant and general differences are attributable to differences of racial composition or anthropologic constitution.

Mr. A. Gehring[1] has drawn such a contrast most skilfully; and, lest I should seem to be affected by any bias of my own, I will follow his lead closely, attempting to give the pith of his observations.

He contrasts the art of the Nordic race with that of the Græco-Latins, in whom the blood of the Mediterranean race predominates. Taking one art after another, he shows that the same essential differences appear. In all arts the classic qualities predominate in the South, the romantic in the North.

The classic qualities are clearness, formality, circumscription, simplicity, directness of appeal to the senses, elegance, symmetry, proportion, observance of the unities of time and place, rationalism, and, I think we may add, a high degree of a quality only recently pointed out as a fundamental quality of works of art, namely, the preservation of what is called " psychical distance "; that is to say, the subject, the topic, is kept remote, more or less unreal, and subordinate, while the essential of success lies in the form of the artist's treatment.[2]

The romantic qualities are the opposite of these —profusion of characters, of qualities, situations, objects and details, and of suggestions of all these things beyond those actually portrayed or presented; complexity of relations, of plot, of design,

[1] " Racial Contrasts," 1908.
[2] *Cf.* " The Æsthetic Attitude," by H. S. Langfeld, 1920.

of emotions , indirectness of appeal, relying upon suggestion of a wealth of imagery and vague meaning, by the figurative and symbolical usage of all material ; the suggestion of mystery, of the unknown and unfathomable ; all prompting, not so much to direct and purely æsthetic enjoyment, as to moral and mystical reflection on man and nature.

To illustrate these differences I will only ask the reader to compare mentally : classical with northern mythology ; a classical temple with a gothic cathedral ; the best Italian painting with works of Rubens, Dürer, Turner, Rembrandt ; Italian music with the music of Wagner and Beethoven ; the classical theatre with the plays of Shakespeare and Goethe's " Faust " ; Homer and Virgil and Horace with Wordsworth, Shelley, Carlyle, Coleridge and Meredith. If we would see the contrast in its full degree, we must compare the greatest works of the greatest artists ; for in these the inward nature of the artist is most truly ànd spontaneously expressed. There are no doubt exceptions (e.g., Michelangelo and Dante[1]) ; but on the whole the contrast is striking and of the same nature in all the arts. Other writers have pointed out the same differences, and some

---

[1] It must be remembered that there was a strong infusion of Nordic blood in northern Italy ; and, though it seems to have left few physical traces at the present time, it was probably more strongly represented at the time of the Renaissance than it is now.

have suggested explanations. M. Boutmy, for example, would attribute the difference to the influence of climate : the mystical, reflective, introspective quality of Northern art to the foggy atmosphere ; the clear, direct appeal to the senses in the South to the clear sunny atmosphere.[1] This is hardly an adequate explanation. For we see that, when a predominantly Nordic people, such as the English, transfers itself to another climate, to New England, where it enjoys a latitude and a brilliant climate comparable to those of southern Europe, it continues in its art to exhibit the same peculiarities ; they are nowhere more strongly presented than in the works of Emerson and Whitman and of other American writers. If climate has anything to do with the production of the difference, the effects of climate must have become impressed on the mind, transmissible and hereditary, through many generations of influence.

Mr. Gehring discerningly remarks : " It is conceivable that vast differences in national activities and institutions are the results of insignificant divergences of mental structure." This is, I think, very true, if we insert the word *seemingly* before " insignificant divergences of mental structure." Is it possible to point to any divergence of mental structure between the Mediterranean and the Nordic races which would explain wholly or in part these wide differences of expression in art ? What constitutional innate differences do

[1] " La psychologie du peuple anglais."

these express ? And can we find other differences of activity which seem to express the same divergence of mental structure or moral endowment ? In seeking such innate differences we may properly turn to the instinctive endowment. We have recently come to recognize, thanks chiefly to William James, that human nature comprises a number of distinct instinctive tendencies or instincts ; that these, though deeply hidden and disguised in the adult man, are nevertheless the mainsprings of all our activities, bodily, emotional and intellectual ; that one man differs from another in the native strength of these several instincts.[1] And, though it seems clear that the same instincts are common to the whole human species, it may be that one race differs from another (statistically) in respect of the relative strengths of the several instincts.

In seeking an explanation along this line, we must not postulate a special instinct as the underlying ground of every special form of national activity, as the literary historians too often have done.[2] We may only invoke, for our historical

---

[1] *Cf.* my " Introduction to Social Psychology," where the part of instincts in human life is discussed at length.

[2] Renan was the great exponent of this *ad hoc* invention of instincts, this facile mode of explanation of historical facts ; e.g., in his polemic against the Jews, he asserted that they were devoid of the instincts for mythology, for polytheism, for epic, for drama, for politics, and for military organization. He never stopped to inquire whether any people possess such instincts, nor even to ask what he meant by the word " instinct."

explanations, instincts which on other grounds we have found reason to believe to be common to the whole human race, and which conform to the psychological and biological conception of instinct.

Let us notice first how some great critics have endeavoured to define the essence of the romantic quality in art. Walter Pater said : " It is the addition of strangeness to beauty that constitutes the romantic character in art ; and the desire of beauty being a fixed element in every artistic . organization, it is the addition of *curiosity* to this desire of beauty that constitutes the romantic temper." Another critic gives substantially the same definition of the romantic. " If we analyse the feeling we shall find, I think, that it has its origin in wonder and mystery. It is the sense of something hidden, of imperfect revelation." (Hedge.)

Curiosity or wonder, then, seems to be the essence of the romantic. Now, curiosity, with the emotion of wonder which enters as an essential element into all such emotions as awe, admiration and reverence, seems to be due to the working within us of a true primitive instinct.[1] If we assume that this instinct is stronger in the Nordic than in the Mediterranean race, we shall have an hypothesis which will partly explain the difference between their arts ; namely, it will largely explain the romantic quality of Northern art. Is there any

[1] *Cf*.my " Social Psychology," pp. 57, 129, and Chapter XIII.

other difference which fits this assumption ? Curiosity or wonder may, without exaggeration, be called the mother of philosophy and of science. Now modern science is very largely a product of northern Europe, of those countries where the Nordic blood predominates ; not exclusively so by any means. But note this fact : the Greeks, who founded philosophy and science, were probably, in their great age, compounded of the Nordic and the Mediterranean races. The Romans were almost purely Mediterranean. They produced great men, great lawyers, soldiers, administrators, and poets ; but no philosophy and no science. For four hundred years they ruled absolutely the fairest part of the world, in a state of high civilization ; but they invented nothing, discovered nothing, made no progress in science. Otto Seeck, the historian of the decay of the classical world, has drawn a vivid picture of this scientific stagnation.[1] He points out how even in the art of war, on success in which their whole empire was founded and maintained, the Romans made no progress, invented no new weapons, but fought in the same old way with the same old weapons throughout the centuries of their predominance. Note another indication of the weakness of their curiosity. In spite of their supremacy, their high civilization, their navy and mercantile marine, they remained a Mediterranean power : their sailors penetrated hardly, if at all, beyond the Pillars of Hercules ;

[1] " Geschichte des Untergangs der antiken Welt."

while the barbarous Vikings in their smaller ships sailed to Iceland, Greenland, and America. Here, then, is further evidence that in the Mediterranean race the instinct of curiosity is relatively weak. But wonder, if it is the mother of science, is also an essential element in religion, entering, as I said, into the religious emotions of awe, admiration, and reverence. It follows that, if our hypothesis is correct, we should expect to find some appreciable difference between the religions of Northern and Southern Europe. To that topic I will return.[1]

Let us pursue further the differences revealed in art. For the hypothesis of a stronger dose of curiosity in the Nordic race will only partially explain these differences. Are there indications of a similar difference between the Mediterranean and the Nordic races in respect of any other of the human instincts ? I seem to see clear indications of one other such difference. The Southern Europeans are more sociable than the Northern. They delight in conversation, in coming together in large masses, in expressing their emotions collectively, in great collective outbursts of applause, of admiration or of execration. In all ages their civilization has been essentially an urban civilization ; they are naturally urbane ; the city has always been their natural habitat.

[1] My friend, Mr. Gilbertson, has drawn my attention to the fact that in some of the Norse folk-tales the younger brother triumphs over his scornful elders by reason of his insatiable curiosity. A very significant fact.

94

Men of Nordic race, on the other hand, are taciturn; they take part in social gatherings only with difficulty and hesitation; they are content to live alone in the seclusion of the family circle, emerging from it only in response to the call of duty or ambition or war. The isolated home is their invention, their dearest possession; and the individualized family home is one of their peculiar contributions to the culture of the world.[1] The facts are all summed up in the phrase—"An Englishman's home is his castle." This difference runs through every form and detail of social life and organization. We may safely infer that it is the expression of an innate difference of constitution.

What is it, then, that impels men to gather together without ulterior purpose, to shrink from isolation as the most intolerable of evils, to find satisfaction in merely being together *en masse*? It is the working of a distinct and now generally recognized instinct, common to the human species and all the gregarious mammals; it is the impulse of the gregarious or herd instinct. We have, it seems, good reason to add to our hypothesis the assumption that this herd instinct is relatively weak in the Nordic, strong in the Mediterranean, peoples. We now have a fuller explanation of the differences between the arts of the two peoples. The art of the Mediterraneans is essentially and most characteristically public art, the art of the

[1] *Cf.* "Histoire de la formation particulariste," by Henri de Tourville. Paris, 1905.

theatre, of the orator, sculpture, architecture, and poetry for public recitation at festivals ; and worship is essentially a public, formal, ritualistic act. Their art is, in all its forms, markedly objective and conventional ; and " conventional " means that it observes generally recognized rules which render it easily intelligible to the masses.

The art of the North, on the other hand, is subjective, individual, peculiar, defying or ignoring all conventions. And the arts most characteristic of the North are reflective nature poetry and the novel or romance which reflectively portrays and analyses character ; both, you see, forms of art fit to be enjoyed only in isolation, by the brooding reader who is content to be moved to laughter or to tears in solitude.

The Nordic race, then, is more curious and less sociable than the Mediterranean. In it the instinct of curiosity is stronger, the herd instinct is weaker. But still we do not seem to have an hypothesis capable of explaining fully the divergences of Northern from Southern art. The vividness and directness of appeal of Southern art, its more passionate, more sensuous quality, still require explanation. These qualities we may naturally associate with a universally recognized difference between the peoples who have created these arts. The Mediterranean peoples are vivacious, quick, impetuous, impulsive ; their emotions blaze out vividly and instantaneously into violent expression and violent action. The Northern peoples are slow, reserved, unexpressive ;

their emotions seem to escape in bodily expression and action with difficulty. If we recognize this as a constitutional difference between the Mediterranean and the Nordic races, we complete the hypothesis needed for the explanation of their divergences in art.

But can we form any valid conception of such a constitutional difference? It is sometimes assumed that in the Southern peoples the emotions and their impulses are inherently stronger than in the Northern. This seems to me entirely fallacious. If it were true, we should except to find the Northern peoples comparatively inert, placid, sluggish, inactive. But see what they have done : their restless energy is chiefly responsible for the transformation of the modern world ; they primarily have peopled North America and Australia, governed India, penetrated to the heart of Africa, settled in every island of Malaysia and the Pacific Ocean, scaled almost all the great mountains and reached the North and the South Poles.

It is obvious that no difference in the relative strength of any instinct could account for the difference we are now considering ; for the difference finds expression in all emotions and in all modes of activity. It seems to be a perfectly general difference of constitution ; whereas all instincts are more or less specific.

Well, modern medicine comes to our help and suggests the true explanation. The modern psychological study of the so-called nervous disorders has

7   97

shown that the functional nervous disorders are really of mental origin, and that they fall into two distinct groups, of which hysteria and neurasthenia are the types, respectively. Now it is found that men and women who break down under nervous strain or emotional shocks tend to develop symptoms of the one or the other kind, according as they belong to one or other of two constitutional types. We owe the clear distinction of these two types to Doctor C. G. Jung of Zurich.[1] He calls them the extrovert and the introvert types. The well-marked extroverts are those whose emotions flow out easily into bodily expression and action. They are the vivid, vivacious, active persons who charm us by their ease and freedom of expression, their frankness, their quick sympathetic responses. They are little given to introspective brooding; they remain relatively ignorant of themselves; for they are essentially objective, they are interested directly and primarily in the outer world about them. When and if they break down under strain, their trouble takes on the hysteric type, the form of dissociations, paralyses, anæsthesias, amnesias; in spite of which they may remain cheerful, active, and interested in the world.

The introvert, on the other hand, is slow and reserved in the expression of his emotions. He has difficulty in adequately expressing himself. His nervous and mental energies, instead of flowing out freely to meet and play upon the outer world,

[1] "Analytic Psychology."

seem apt to turn inward, determining him to brooding, reflection, deliberation before action. And, when he is subject to strain, his energies are absorbed in internal conflicts ; he becomes dead to the outer world, languid, absorbed, self-centred, and full of vague distress.

This difference of constitutional type is not due to difference of environment and training. Within the same family you may see well-marked examples of both types, though all have been subjected to almost identical environmental influences. The difference between the two types seems to be the expression of a subtle difference of physiological constitution which pervades every part of the nervous system. What exactly it consists in we do not know. Many years ago I threw out an hypothesis as to the nature of this peculiarity of nervous constitution and I believe it is essentially correct or on the right lines. But it is too technical a matter to discuss here. Suffice it to say that it seems to explain the facts, and the suggested peculiarity is one which may well be transmitted hereditarily.[1]

Physicians who have specialized in nervous disorders in both the North and the South of Europe assure me that the Northerners are much more commonly subject to the neurasthenic type of trouble, the Southerners to the hysteric type. This fits exactly with the universally recognized difference between North and South.

[1] " The Conditions of Fatigue in the Nervous System," *Brain*, Vol. XXXII. 1909.

We may fairly complete our hypothesis by assuming that the Mediterranean race is constitutionally extrovert, the Nordic race constitutionally introvert. Of course, exceptions may occur ; the statement can be only statistically true ; and especially, in view of the fact of the wide mixture of blood of the two races, and the peculiar mixture of innate qualities that results from race blending, we may expect many mixed and ill-defined types ; which is what we actually find.

We seem now to have completed our hypothesis for the explanation of the divergence of the North from the South of Europe in respect of their artistic expressions. The Nordic race is constitutionally introvert ; it is strong in the instinct of curiosity, the root of wonder ; weak in the herd instinct, the root of sociability. In the Mediterranean race these peculiarities are reversed ; it is extrovert, weak in curiosity, strong in sociability.

If our hypothesis is correct, we should expect to find other differences between North and South to the explanation of which it may be applied.[1]

[1] One such striking difference, which may be noted in passing, is the greater proneness to alcoholic intoxication of the Nordic peoples and the great sobriety in this respect of the Mediterranean peoples. Sir Archdall Reid (in his " Present Evolution of Man ") has argued that the greater sobriety of the populations of the South of Europe is the consequence of their longer usage of alcoholic liquors, which he supposes to have weeded out from them all strains peculiarly susceptible to their influence. It seems to me more probable that the explanation is to be found in the introvert quality of the Nordic race. Alcohol acts

In discussing art it was possible to leave out of our view the third great race which has contributed a full share of its blood to the population of modern Europe, namely, the Alpine race, which geographically occupies, or predominates in, the middle zone. For the art of this race (the art of the Slavs, and that generally known as Celtic) has been somewhat apart from the two great rival traditions, the classical and the romantic. But at this point we must bring this race into our discussion. It must suffice to say that, in both physical and mental qualities, it seems to stand between the Mediterranean and the Nordic races. Physically, it is distinguished from the Mediterranean race by having a round rather than a long head. Mentally, it seems to be introvert rather than extrovert, but not so extremely introvert as the Nordic race. It has in common with the Mediterranean race a high degree of sociability; and is, I think, though here I speak less confidently, like it, relatively weak in curiosity.

The Nordic race is, then, to be distinguished physically from the other two races by fair hair and complexion and by high stature. And it seems to be unlike both of them in respect of the three mental qualities we have defined. These two

on the nervous system in a way which renders it temporarily extrovert; and thus for the introvert it brings relief from the brooding melancholy to which he is constitutionally liable; it enables him to enjoy the freedom of emotional expression which in his normal condition is denied him by his introvert constitution.

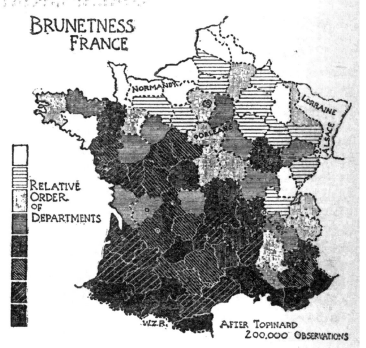

BRUNETNESS
FRANCE

NORMANDY

LORRAINE

ORLEANS

ALSACE

RELATIVE
ORDER.
OF
DEPARTMENTS

W.Z.R.

AFTER TOPINARD
200,000 OBSERVATIONS

physical qualities serve as the indicators of the
blood of this race ; and maps of the physical qualities of the European peoples show clearly the
regions of its predominance. There are maps
which reveal a similar distribution of mental or
moral peculiarities. I will put before you some
maps which show the distribution of certain
physical and moral traits.

The first map shows that fair complexion predominates in the north-eastern part of France, and
that this area of " fairness " is prolonged in two

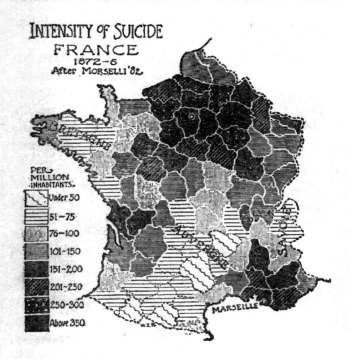

INTENSITY of SUICIDE
FRANCE
1872-6
After MORSELLI '82.

PER
MILLION
INHABITANTS.

Under 50
51-75
76-100
101-150
151-200
201-250
250-300
Above 350

directions, namely south-westward to Bordeaux and southward along the valley of the Rhone. The map of the distribution of stature agrees closely with this, showing predominance of tall stature in the same regions.[1] Historical and archæological evidence shows that these are the regions in which the Nordic tribes established themselves most fully, driving out or extermin-

[1] *Cf.* Professor Z. Ripley's " Races of Europe." I am indebted to Professor Ripley for his permission to reproduce these maps.

ating in large measure their forerunners of Alpine and Mediterranean race

Now examine the map showing the relative frequency of suicide in the provinces of modern France. It is obvious that this map corresponds very closely with the other. Wherever the physical marks (fair complexion and high stature) of the Nordic race predominate, there suicide is frequent, and conversely.

The suggestion is that suicide is frequent in proportion to the predominance of Nordic blood E. Morselli (the Italian alienist) has pointed out this correlation and has deduced the conclusion that the Nordic race is more apt at suicide than the other European races. Cautious anthropologists (including Professor Ripley, from whose valuable book on " The Races of Europe " I have copied these maps) have refused to follow him. It is necessary to be something of a psychologist, perhaps, if one is to appreciate the evidence. For other men of science, even the medical men, are systematically trained to ignore the mind of man. For them it is something unreal, because intangible. They are willing to attribute such a phenomenon as the prevalence of suicide in an area to climate, or diet, or geological formation, or the electric disturbances of the atmosphere, for all these are " real." But to attribute it to mental peculiarities or conditions seems to them pure mythology.

Well, Morselli traced and mapped the frequency

of suicide in all parts of Europe. It must be admitted that he relied too much upon language as a criterion of race ; and he showed very convincingly that there is a very high correlation between suicide and the use of the German language, that those who speak German are very apt to commit suicide. Some readers may at once infer that the language is the cause of the suicide; and perhaps it would be difficult completely to refute such a simple and attractive theory. But, looking at the facts more widely, we see that the frequency of suicide is correlated not only, or chiefly, with language, but rather with the physical qualities of the Nordic race. Take France ; the correlation is close. Professor Ripley sugests it is due to the fact that the Nordics occupy the regions of greatest industrial activity and prosperity, where larger towns are frequent. But that they occupy these regions is a fact which in turn requires explanation. Turn, then, to another detailed map—that of England.

Notice that there are three regions in which suicide is least frequent, namely Wales, Cornwall, and an area lying a little to the north of London. All three are areas in which the Nordic blood is but little represented. The Welsh represent the pre-Saxon population, with little admixture of Nordic blood ; and that they are mentally very different from the English is a fact of common knowledge. Very striking is the contrast between Cornwall and Devonshire. Every summer visitor to these counties

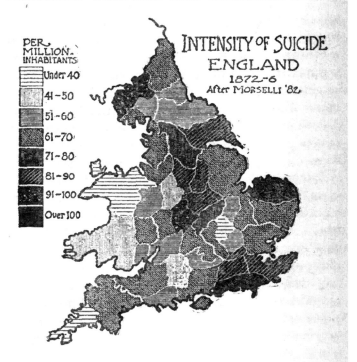

PER
MILLION
INHABITANTS:
Under 40
41-50
51-60
61-70
71-80
81-90
91-100
Over 100

INTENSITY OF SUICIDE
ENGLAND
1872-6
After MORSELLI '82

notices the very marked mental differences between their populations. Devonshire is a typically English county. Its population has played a prominent part in many of the most characteristically English activities, especially in sea-roving, in colonial adventure, in pioneering. It is the traditional home of the English "sea-kings." The population of Cornwall, like that of Wales, is in the main descended from the British tribes which were driven westward by the Anglo-Saxon invaders. Among them the ancient British language has only recently died out. In respect of all other conditions, the two counties are extremely similar, save that Devonshire is rather more fertile. Both are predominantly agricultural and pastoral and seafaring, with an equable mild climate. Yet, as regards the frequency of suicide, we see the large difference indicated by the map. Perhaps even more striking is the small area north of London. The physical anthropologists have shown that, owing to circumstances not fully understood, the population of this region shows predominance of the physical qualities of the pre-English or British tribes. It seems to be an island of the old British population, surrounded by, but not displaced or swamped by, the tide of Anglo-Saxon invasion. And in this small island of population, the physical and economic conditions of which differ hardly appreciably from those of the surrounding counties, suicide remains at its lowest rate, namely, that of Wales and Cornwall.

On the other hand, suicide reaches its highest rate in Sussex, the population of which county is perhaps the most purely and typically Saxon of all England.

Now consider Table V (see next page).

It will be seen that suicide is most frequent in the Scandinavian countries, those of which the population is most purely Nordic; moderately high in England and South Australia, where the population shows a fair proportion of the physical qualities of the Nordic race. The rate is very

TABLE V

ANNUAL SUICIDES PER MILLION POPULATION [1]

Denmark	268
Scandinavia	127
N. Germany	150
S. Germany	165
England	72
S. Australia	90
Wales	52
Ireland	10
Spain	17
Russia	30
N. Italy	46
S. Italy	26

low in Ireland, in spite of all the political troubles and economic distress of her people ; and very low in Spain, South Italy, and Russia, where the Nordic blood is scarce.

In view of all these facts, we can hardly doubt that the racial hypothesis contains much truth. Of course, other factors than race are important. Germany, north and south, has undue pre-eminence ; it may be due to language or government or other lack of harmony. But the facts, taken all together, do strongly support the racial hypothesis. And they do so the more strongly if we take into consideration the following facts. Suicide is a form of violence, of homicide ; we might, then, on superficial consideration, expect to find suicide most frequent where other forms of violence and of homicide abound. The truth is just the converse of this expectation. It is in Southern

[1] This table is extracted from E. Morselli's " Le Suicide."

Italy, Corsica, and Sardinia, where the population is most purely Mediterranean, that crimes of violence, especially homicide, are most frequent; while suicide is very infrequent. Further, suicide is three to four times as frequent among men as among women in all peoples. It is fourteen times as frequent among the whites of New York State as among the coloured population, proportionately to their numbers. Can this be attributed to social advantages enjoyed by women all over the world, or by the coloured people of New York ? No, it is constitutional. The racial hypothesis is immensely strengthened, when we see that these peculiar features of the distribution of suicide and homicide are in perfect harmony with the conclusions we have drawn from the comparison of the arts of Northern and Southern Europe; they are just what we should expect, if the three European races differ in mental constitution in the ways assumed by our hypothesis.

But, before dwelling on this, let us glance at yet another moral peculiarity which still further strengthens the argument, namely the frequency of divorce. Maps of the frequency of divorce or separation in Europe show a close correlation of high frequency of divorce with the physical qualities of the Nordic race. The relation is disturbed by religious influences. But take France. We see that high frequency of divorce and separation occurs in the same areas in which suicide and the physical qualities of the Nordic race abound.

Well, the introvert and unsociable race is the

one prone to suicide and divorce. The sociable and extrovert race is prone to homicide, but not to divorce or suicide. Is not this in accordance with the mental peculiarities which on other grounds we have assigned to the two races? We know that the introvert tends to brood over his difficulties; he readily becomes a prey to internal conflict of the emotions; and, as a matter of fact, such conflict does not only give rise to nervous disorder of the neurasthenic type, but, in not a few of these cases, leads on to suicide. As regards divorce, we may suppose that the injured Nordic, the unsociable introvert, broods over his wrongs, and then, nursing his resentment, either seeks redress in the law courts or deserts his partner and becomes liable to be divorced for desertion. In the impulsive sociable extrovert, on the other hand, the emotion of anger blazes out, passes at once to action and often to homicide; and, when he is injured by the unfaithfulness of his partner, he does not brood upon the problem—he solves it at once by using knife or pistol upon one or both of the guilty parties.

Perhaps it is not fantastic to suggest that our third point of difference also tends in the same direction. The curious Nordic, we may suppose, brooding in secret distress and pondering the problem of his partner's infidelity, strives to understand how such an act has become possible: while for the impetuous incurious Mediterranean the fact alone suffices; his hand is not arrested by

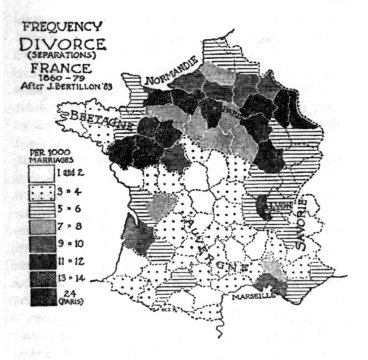

FREQUENCY
DIVORCE
(SEPARATIONS)
FRANCE
1860 – 79
After J. BERTILLON '83

PER 1000
MARRIAGES
1 and 2
3 » 4
5 » 6
7 » 8
9 » 10
11 » 12
13 » 14
24
(PARIS)

any desire to understand the conditions which have produced it.

Even in suicide curiosity may play its part, Is not death a great adventure into the unknown? May not the desire to know the last secret have urged some reflective and unhappy souls, exasperated by the mystery of human life, to penetrate by their own act the impenetrable veil?

I will pass very quickly over another allied topic, the distribution of the forms of religion. The distribution of all the great religions of the world presents interesting and suggestive questions of race, especially perhaps Buddhism, which, after rising and spreading rapidly in India, passed equally rapidly away eastward, to become enduringly established among all branches of the yellow race. But I will keep nearer home and insist only on the distribution of Protestantism and of Roman and Greek Catholicism, the three great religious forms of Europe. The suggestion that this is largely a matter of race is not new. It has often been made and often denied. In the main the two forms of Catholicism are religions of authority, of convention, of ritual; they are preeminently social in their rites and celebrations. Only the Protestant reads his Bible in his closet and communes alone with God, pondering the problems of life and death. Only the Protestant Church has split into a thousand peculiar sects, each maintaining its peculiar creed and practice; and only Protestants have traversed wide oceans in search of lands where they might worship God after their own fashion. Or, rather, Protestantism is the only one of the three forms which permits and even encourages such individualism and independence.

Now, of course, the vast majority of men grow up in and adhere to the church of their fathers. But the Protestants did, as a matter of historical fact, break away from the Church of Rome; and those who have broken away are in the main just those peoples and those sections of nations in which the physical qualities of the Nordic race predominate; while all those in which the other two races clearly predominate have remained subject to the Catholic Church of East or West. Among the former are the populations of Northern France, Holland, Denmark, Scandinavia, Finland, England, of most of Scotland, and of Northern Germany. Ireland, the western Highlands, Southern France and Germany, and all to the south and east of them remain subject to the religions of authority. There are exceptions to the rule, e.g., Wales, Cornwall, parts of Belgium and of Switzerland ; and it is true that some of the great reformers belonged to Switzerland.[1] But the other influences have played a part.

Is it, then, mere coincidence that the peoples in which predominates the blood of the curious, inquiring, unsociable, reflective, introvert Nordic race, and these only, with few small exceptions, have broken away from the religions of authority, of convention, of formal ritual, of outward action and emotional display ? The historian may point to the personal and political circumstances of the reign of Henry VIII of England, or suggest a score of alternative explanations from the depths of his learning. But he seems to me to ask too much of our credulity, if he would ascribe the whole correlation to a multitude of historical accidents.

In this connection I would insist upon the im-

[1] Calvin, it is said, was of northern French descent.

portance of a principle which I have enunciated in my " Group Mind."[1] It is this.. The innate mental qualities of any stably organized people or nation are revealed more clearly in the national character and in the national institutions than in the characters of individuals. For the character of each individual is very greatly moulded by the national institutions and traditions among which he grows up ; to such an extent, in fact, that his native disposition may seem to be swamped, overlaid, and totally obscured by the tendencies acquired through training, imitation, and social pressure of all sorts. But the culture of each of the modern nations has been slowly built up, partly by original invention, but more largely by absorption of elements imitated from other nations. Of the family of nations each contributes something to a common stock of culture derived by tradition from the past ; from this common stock each nation selects what best suits its people, and, having adopted such an element, modifies it to suit its own nature more exactly. Thus the culture, the sum of the traditions and institutions, of each nation, grows in an environment which exerts constantly a selective and moulding influence upon it ; just as, according to the Darwinian theory, the various species of animals have become slowly differentiated and evolved by the selective and moulding action of their environments. In the case of the national culture-species, the environment which thus selects and moulds

[1] New York, 1920.

the enduring elements is the sum of the native qualities of the people. I would call this *the law of the adaptation of the culture-species.* We may see illustrations of it on every hand. From the operation of this law it results that each nation which has enjoyed a long period of development without serious interruption has acquired traditions and institutions that are in harmony with its predominant native qualities. Therefore, in the development of each member of such a nation, nature and nurture work harmoniously together. Just for this reason it is so difficult to distinguish, in any one member of such a nation, the influence of his native disposition from that of the culture by which his development has been moulded.

This law is of little significance in relation to such peculiarities as the frequency of suicide and divorce. But it is of great importance in relation to all things regulated by legislation and by established custom and tradition, such things as religion and social organization, the form of the family, the village community, land tenure, political and educational institutions.

Bearing this law in mind, let us examine what appears to be a particularly instructive instance of a large difference in the destinies of two peoples, determined by a small difference of anthropologic constitution.

I refer to the French and the British nations. Both stand in the van of Western civilization ; both have produced many men of the first order in many spheres of activity. Each inhabits a beautiful, rich, and fertile country, of temperate climate, well placed geographically in every regard, cultural, climatic, commerical, military. In all these respects the French nation has, if anything, the advantage of the British.

Both nations have been great conquerors and colonists. Yet how different at the present time are their positions as world influences! The French have conquered and ruled immense areas of the surface of the earth. Yet nowhere outside France is there any large community of people of French descent and speech living under the French flag ; nowhere save in Canada any considerable population of French descent.[1] And France's tenure of those great colonial territories over which she now rules seems to be comparatively precarious and uncertain. Britain, on the other hand, not only administers the affairs of one-fifth of the people of the world, but has peopled North America and Australia, and keeps under her flag immense territories inhabited by her sons. And, while the French language and traditions seem to have small prospect of a future outside France, the English language and British traditions seem to be in a fair way to prevail increasingly throughout the world. Further, in nearly all her great colonial adventures—in

[1] It is said that approximately 1,000,000 of the population of the French possessions in North Africa are of French descent. This is to be set over against the millions of Australasia, Canada, and South Africa.

India, in Canada, in Louisiana, in the West Indies, in China, in Africa—France has come into rivalry with the British and has been worsted.

Is all this great divergence of destiny due to a converging series of historical accidents ? Or is there one underlying cause or condition ? May we not fairly seek the ground of this difference of destiny in some difference of anthropologic constitution of the two nations ? The key to the problem seems to me to have been given in a passage written long ago by a French traveller in North America, Volney. He contrasts the French with the British colonist as follows : " The French colonist deliberates with his wife upon everything that he proposes to do ; often the plans fall to the ground through lack of agreement. . . . To visit one's neighbours, to chat with them, is for the French an habitual need so imperious that on all the frontier of Louisiana and Canada you will not find a single French colonist established beyond sight of his neighbour's home. . . . On the other hand, the English colonist, slow and taciturn, passes the whole day continuously at work ; at breakfast he coldly gives his orders to his wife . . . and goes forth to labour. If he finds an opportunity to sell his farm at a profit, he does so and goes ten or twenty leagues farther into the wilderness to make himself a new home."

There we have, I suggest, the key to the difference we are examining. And this testimony does not stand alone. It is in harmony with a great number of social differences presented by the two peoples ; the centralized form of government in France as against the local autonomies of Britain ; the form of the French family and the laws and customs regulating family life, e.g., the laws of inheritance ; the educational system as against the English lack of educational system ; the predominance of co-operative centrally organized activities among the French ; the individual enterprise and lack of systematic organization of the British.[1] All these and other similar differences have been pointed out and dwelt upon by many French writers [2]; and various attempts have been made to explain them as the result of historical events, such as the more thorough Romanization of Gaul, the conquest of England by William of Normandy, the different operation of the feudal system in the two countries. T. H. Buckle was one of those who dwelt upon these differences and who claimed to explain them from such historical episodes. He summed up the difference in two convenient phrases, the predominance of the spirit of protection in France and the predominance of the spirit of independence in Britain.

[1] The difference is strikingly illustrated by the Romanized and codified law of France and the chaotic common law of England, which is dominated by judge-made precedents. I understand from Dean Roscoe Pound that the law of England only narrowly escaped Romanization at one period, thanks to the independent spirit of some English lawyers.

[2] See especially Ed. Demolin's " A quoi tient la supériorité des Anglo-Saxons ? "

I will not delay to examine these proposed explanations and to show you their inadequacy. I have done so elsewhere.[1] I will only remark that so general a phenomenon requires for its explanation a general deep-lying cause, such as is only to be found in some difference of native qualities between the two peoples.

Let us compare the two peoples in respect of racial composition as revealed by history and by physical anthropology. The French people seems to have been formed by a mixture and partial blending of the three great European races in approximately equal proportions. The British people seems to have been formed chiefly by a mixture and partial blending of the Nordic and the Mediterranean races ; the Alpine, which probably predominates in France numerically, being hardly represented, and the Nordic predominating over the other elements. Probably most anthropologists would assign Nordic blood to Britain to the extent of 60 or 70 per cent., the rest being largely Mediterranean ; and to France some 25 per cent. Nordic blood, with perhaps 40 per cent. Alpine and 35 per cent. Mediterranean. This is a very rough estimate, of course.

We may ask : Given the moral peculiarities of the Nordic race which we have inferred on other grounds, does this considerably greater proportion of the blood and the qualities of that race suffice to account for the contrast between the two nations

[1] " The Group Mind."

expressed by Buckle's phrase—the predominance
of the spirit of protection in France and of the
spirit of independence in Britain ? It does, I think,
go some way to explain it ; especially if we note that
sociability or gregariousness, which we saw to be
strong in the Mediterranean race, is at least as strong,
perhaps stronger, in the Alpine. We have seen
from Volney's description how the sociability of
the Frenchman handicaps him, as compared with
the Briton, when he becomes a pioneer and colonist
in new lands.

We may suppose also that the greater curiosity
of the Nordic race contributes to give the Briton
that restless wandering habit which has spread him
over all the surface of the earth, so that, no matter
to what remote region one may penetrate, it is likely
that some solitary Briton will presently appear
and casually borrow a copy of the London *Times*.

CHAPTER V

HAVING found reasons for assigning certain qualities to the three great races of Europe, we are attempting to apply this hypothesis to the explanation of that striking difference between the French and British nations which is summed up in the phrase—the prevalence in France of the spirit of protection, in Britain of the spirit of independence.

We saw that the greater sociability of the French, which I attributed to the greater strength of the gregarious impulse in the Mediterranean and Alpine races, goes some way to explain this difference; and that the stronger curiosity of the Nordic race would also contribute to it.

But the differences between the institutions and customs of the two peoples at home and abroad seem to require the assumption of a further difference of innate quality. The Briton's intolerance of authority, his dislike of being controlled, governed, administered, and his preference for individual initiative, show themselves in all his conduct of affairs; they are well expressed in the accepted dictum that the British, when engaged in any large enterprise, " muddle through " somehow. They have always had to " muddle through," because they will not submit to being deliberately organized and led, according to any logically thought-out scheme. The first partial exception in their history was the acceptance of compulsory military service under the extreme pressure of the Great War.

The French, on the other hand, have always been ready to accept organization and leadership, to look for it to the State or to some man of dominating personality—a Napoleon, a Gambetta, a Boulanger, or a Richelieu.

We may note in passing that this tendency to seek personal leadership seems to be still stronger in the Germans, among whom the Alpine blood is even more strongly represented than in the French. Their docility under an autocratic and arbitrary bureaucracy ; their suggestibility in all matters of belief ; their devotion to the Kaiser (which even now threatens to restore him to the throne) ; the flourishing of a host of little princes and grand dukes ; the spirit of caste, which leads each man to seek a definite position in the official hierarchy and from it to look up humbly to all above him in the scale—all these are significant of a society in which a docile race is dominated by one of a more self-assertive quality.[1] This actually and historically

[1] The organization of Germany for her bid for world domination seems to have been in the main the work of the Prussian aristocracy, the Junkers, a class in which the Nordic blood preponderates. The tendency of the masses of the German people to proclaim " Deutschland über Alles " is a recent phenomenon, induced and sedulously

is, I suggest, the condition of affairs in Germany and the key to its history ; and to a less degree it is true of France also.

The history of the purest stocks of the Nordic race illustrates abundantly and overwhelmingly their lack of docility, their possession in the highest degree of the opposite quality of self-assertion, exhibiting itself as initiative, enterprise, impatience of control. The Normans, a pure Nordic stock, exhibited this quality in a truly marvellous degree in their great age, when they conquered northern France, all England, Sicily, and much of Italy and of the Mediterranean coasts. For these astonishing feats were accomplished, not by the power of great highly organized states and immense armies of conscripts, slaves, or mercenaries, but by small bands of volunteers associated together for each

---

cultivated in their docile minds by the official hierarchy. Bismarck said : " The preponderance of dynastic attachment and the use of a dynasty as the indispensable cement to hold together a definite portion of the nation calling itself by the name of the dynasty is a specific peculiarity of the German Empire " (" Bismarck, the Man and the Statesman," Vol. I, p. 322. Butter).

The late German Emperor is reported to have proclaimed : " There is only one master of the nation. And that is I, and I will not abide any other." . . . " I need Christian soldiers, soldiers who say their Pater Noster. The soldier should not have a will of his own, but you should all have but one will and that is my will ; there is but one law for you, and that is mine." The English nation quickly resented the claim to the divine right of kings, and settled the question promptly and finally, very soon after the " right " was proclaimed to it.

particular enterprise under some chosen leader.

The anthropologists of the school of Le Play have offered a most interesting theory of the origin in prehistoric times of this very marked difference between the Nordic and the Alpine race.[1] Whatever its origin, it must, I think, be accepted as one of the clearest and most important differences of racial quality. Are there, then, any recognized factors in human nature which may be the innate basis of this difference ?

I have shown[2] that docility and self-assertion are rooted in two distinct and opposed instinctive tendencies, which I have proposed to call the instincts of submission and of self-assertion respectively. I have shown reason to believe that the former is the root of all docility and suggestibility, that it is the principal factor in all those social phenomena which some authors have erroneously ascribed to the herd instinct.[3] And I have shown that the other, the instinct of self-assertion, is the most essential, the all-important factor in what we call character, that complex organization from which spring all manifestations of will-power, all volition, resolution, hard choice, initiative, enterprise, determination.

If, then, we add to the qualities already assigned to the Nordic race an exceptional degree of strength

[1] I have given a condensed account of this theory in my " Group Mind."

[2] In my " Introduction to Social Psychology."

[3] E.g., W. Trotter, in " Instincts of the Herd in Peace and War."

of this instinct of self-assertion, and attribute to the Alpine race a stronger instinct of submission, we complete our hypothetical description of their racial qualities in a way which solves our present problem. It is this greater dose of self-assertiveness in the Briton which leads other peoples to complain that he goes about the world as though it belonged to him ; it is this which, in spite of his lack of method and organization, has enabled him to " muddle through " the Napoleonic Wars, the Crimean War, the Indian Mutiny, the South African War, and, lastly, the Great War. It is this which, in spite of his lack of subtlety and sympathy and intellectuality, has enabled him to subdue and govern the 300,000,000 of India. And it is this, in combination with the other Nordic qualities noted in the foregoing pages, that has rendered him the successful colonist *par excellence.*

Let us note in passing that the addition of this quality to the picture of the Nordic race completes, or makes more adequate, our explanation of the distribution of the Protestant religion in the world ; for it shows us that the men of this race are by nature Protestants, essentially protesters and resisters against every form of domination and organization, whether by despot, church, or state.

Now consider for a moment the question of differences of innate moral qualities between more widely unlike races. We have found evidence of such moral differences where there is no evidence of differences of intellectual level, and between races closely allied and of similar civilizations. Is it not probable that, between races which show marked differences of intellectual capacity and which, in physical qualities and in level and type of culture, are widely different, there may be still larger differences of innate moral qualities? I think it is highly probable. But I do not feel competent to say much on this head. One would need an intimate acquaintance with extra-European civilizations, such as I cannot claim.

I would point out that, in respect of the peoples which have evolved no distinctive culture of their own, any reply to this question is peculiarly difficult; just because they lack the developed traditions and institutions which, as I have argued, give the best and clearest expression to the native qualities of any developed nation. But consider a single striking instance of such difference of moral quality—the difference between the Red man and the Black. Consider the difference of their relations to the Whites throughout the history of America. The Negro has in a way adapted himself to the position imposed upon him. He has multiplied, in spite of the ravages of disease,[1] in both slavery and freedom. But the Red man has never let himself be impressed into the social system of the dominant Whites; in some peculiar way he has proved resistant; he dies rather than submit. Does not this imply some deep-seated moral difference between the two races?

[1] It is well known that alcohol, tuberculosis, and syphilis have taken a heavy toll of both Red and Black.

If the Red man had the adaptability of the Negro, would he not have become a very important factor in the history of the United States of America ? The same difference has appeared clearly throughout the West Indies, where the more adaptable Black race has superseded the Red men even more completely than on the mainland. I am not sufficiently acquainted with the two races to attempt to define the racial qualities which have determined this difference. I will suggest merely, on the basis of a slight knowledge : (1) that the Negro race is pronouncedly extrovert, and that the red men are equally extreme introverts ; (2) that the black race is more strongly gregarious and sociable ; (3) further, that the red race is strongly self-assertive, while in the Negro the submissive impulse is strong. The last point may be illustrated by a true story of a Negro maid, whose Northern mistress, after treating her with great forbearance for a time, in spite of shortcomings, turned upon her and scolded her vigorously. The maid showed no resentment, but rather showed signs of a new satisfaction, and exclaimed : " Lor', Missus, you do make me feel so good." This seems to be a typical and significant incident. I will even venture to suggest that, in the great strength of this instinct of submission, we have the main key to the history of the Negro race. In its own country it has always been ruled by absolute despots, who have obtained the most abject submission from their subjects, even when they have ruled with the utmost cruelty. These despots have often been men of foreign blood, Arabs largely. When Negroes have been well handled, with firmness but with kindness and consideration, as by the French officers who have trained the black regiments of France, they have proved themselves to be capable of extreme courage, devotion, and loyalty, to be, in short, ideal followers.[1]

The extreme facility with which the pure Negroes

[1] *Cf.* "Le Courage," by Voivenel and Huot. Paris, 1918. Shaler (*op. cit.*) insists upon the imitativeness and the eminent faithfulness of the Negroes to their white masters, and upon their sympathetic responsiveness ; they "have the whole range of primitive sympathies exceedingly well developed. They have a singularly quick, sympathetic contact with the neighbour ; they attain to his state of mind and shape themselves to meet him as no other primitive people do. Those who have had a chance to compare in this regard the Negro and the American Indian must have been struck by the difference between the two peoples in this most important feature." Intimate contact with Oceanic Negroes (in the Torres Straits) and with Malays during many months impressed me strongly with the magnitude of this same difference between these outlying branches of these two races. Shaler points also to another striking difference between the black man and the red. He asserts that the Negro is much more capable of sustained labour, and he connects this with the fact that the Negroes have long practised a rude agriculture, while the ancestors of the red men were hunters and nomads. It seems to me doubtful whether this difference is rooted in innate or racial qualities. Any disposition to sustained labour is certainly conspicuous by its absence in the Oceanic Negroes with whom I am acquainted. It is difficult to conceive of such a disposition as an hereditary quality ; this difference between Black and Red in America may well be due to the different conditions of life of the two races in the present and in the recent past.

adopt the most extravagant superstitions, and the great influence of these upon their conduct—these facts point to and support the same assumption, namely, an exceptional strength of the submissive instinct, the root of all docility and suggestibility.

There is a moral difference which distinguishes most of the peoples of primitive culture from those which have developed or acquired civilization ; this, though it is difficult to explain, seems to be of the first importance. It may be defined as the difference between providence and improvidence. Improvidence is marked in the Malay and the Negro, the two tropical races *par excellence ;* in less degree, perhaps, in the peoples of India (it is said that the Hindu family habitually squanders extravagant sums on such ceremonials as weddings and funerals) ; and in the Polynesian, Indonesian, and Melanesian ; in fact, in all the races which have long inhabited the tropic regions, where man can survive without taking much thought for the morrow.

The opposite quality, providence, on the other hand, is shown in a high degree by all the peoples that have developed a high civilization. If we look more closely at these qualities, we see that improvidence is a negative quality ; it is due to the absence of something which makes a man provident. This is not merely a matter of intelligence and imagination. The imagination of the Negro race seems to be vivid and powerful. It may be true that many of the improvident races are of rather low intellectual capacity. But a man may

9   129

be extremely provident, in fact a real miser, in spite of a low degree of intelligence.

If a man is to be provident, he must be so constituted as to find some satisfaction in possession ; that is to say, there must be in him an impulse to save or hoard which finds satisfaction in the act of hoarding, an impulse which prompts him to postpone enjoyment of the pleasure of immediate use to the satisfaction of possession. Such an impulse is shown by many animals, and I have claimed it as a true instinctive tendency of human nature.[1]

The strength or weakness of this tendency is, I suggest, the main factor in determining that a man or a race shall be provident or improvident. And it is very easy to see how natural selection may have developed this quality in peoples inhabiting cold or arid regions. It seems, in fact, to be present in the principal races in proportion to the demand for it made by their habitat. It seems to be strong in the Alpine and the Nordic race and in the Chinese ; less strong in most branches of the Mediterranean ; but strong in the Semites, in the Jews and Arabs and the Phœnicians, who long inhabited the dry desert regions.[2] Its strength seems to be a quality essential to any people that is to build up a civilization based on the accumulation of wealth, on com-

[1] " Social Psychology."
[2] I may add that while writing these pages I have received from Australia a letter informing me of the opinion of the greatest living authority on the black natives of that continent, to the effect that the race is extremely deficient in, or wholly innocent of, the acquisitive impulse.

merce and industry, as every higher civilization has been. Owing to this necessity, every communistic or socialistic scheme which would abolish private property is an empty dream, an unrealizable ideal, a Utopia. The strength of this impulse seems to vary widely even in nearly related peoples, and also from one family to another. It would certainly seem to be stronger in the lowland Scots than in the Irish ; and it is, I think, not improbable that its variations are a principal ground of the social stratification which tends to arise in all acquisitive societies, that is to say, in all civilized peoples.

We have found reason to believe that, though the Nordic race has no monopoly of genius, though it does not excel, and perhaps does not equal, other races in many forms of excellence (as so extravagantly claimed by the race-dogmatists), it yet has certain qualities which have played a great part in determining the history, the institutions, the customs and traditions, and the geographical distribution of the peoples in whom its blood is strongly represented.

· With two exceptions (namely, differences of intellectual stature and those subtle peculiarities of nervous constitution which determine extroversion and introversion) all the peculiarities we have assigned hitherto to races have been degrees of strength of certain instinctive tendencies.

We must ask—Are there other innate inherited qualities, besides these instincts which in their sum and balance are so large a part of the basis of moral development or character ? The answer clearly is —Yes. We know that individuals differ in such things as musical and mathematical talent ; and we know, also, that these talents are hereditary, and that, in respect of musical talent at least, there are marked differences between peoples. For example, no one can question the fact that the Welsh people is (statistically) more musically gifted than the English.

The innate basis of such talents is a very obscure matter ; we do not know whether such a talent is an hereditary unit-quality or not. Probably it is complex. But we really are in almost total ignorance. I mention these special endowments, in order to enforce the contention that the innate basis of the mind may be far richer and more complex than is commonly assumed by the psychologists.

One medical psychologist of great experience and repute, Doctor C. G. Jung, has been led by many years devoted to deep exploration of the minds of nervous patients to believe that the innate basis of the mind comprises much that is specific and differentiated ; he has revived the theory of innate ideas. He believes that each of us inherits what he calls " the collective unconscious," a part of the mind which manifests itself most clearly in dreams and in states of mental disorder, but which colours and biases all our thinking. This " collective unconscious " reveals itself chiefly in certain " archetypes," ideas which have a wide symbolical function, images which stand for or symbolize

132

certain universally recurring relations and problems ,
of human life. He holds that, though certain
older and most fundamental of these " archetypes "
are common to the whole human race, each race
or each people that has lived for many generations
under or by a particular type of civilization has
specialized its " collective unconscious," differentiated and developed the " archetypes " into forms
peculiar to itself.

He claims that in many cases he can discover
the racial origins, the blood, of his patients by
studying the forms of symbolism and the allegorical
figures which appear in their dreams. He claims
even that sometimes a single rich dream has enabled
him to discover the fact, say, of Jewish or Mediterranean blood in a patient who shows none of the outward physical marks of such descent. And he finds
these " archetypes " expressed in the mythology and
folk-lore of each people, as well as in their dreams.[1]

Clearly, if these views of Doctor Jung are well
founded, they are of the first importance for our
topic ; they would carry the doctrine of racial
peculiarities of mental constitution much farther
than I have done so far. The interest and importance of these views has seemed to me so great that
I have put myself into the hands of Doctor Jung
and asked him to explore the depths of my mind,
my " collective unconscious " ; that is to say, having
no well-marked symptoms of insanity or neurosis
which might reveal my " unconscious," I have

[1] *Cf.* his " Psychology of the Unconscious."

assiduously studied my own dreams under his direction and with his help. And the result is— I "evermore came out by that same door wherein I went." I cannot find grounds for a decided opinion. I seem to find in myself traces or indications of Doctor Jung's "archetypes," but faint and doubtful traces. Perhaps it is that I am too mongrel-bred to have clear-cut archetypes ; perhaps my "collective unconscious"—if I have one—is mixed and confused and blurred. One of Jung's arguments weighs with me a good deal in favour of his view. He points out that the famous theory of Freud, which he himself at one time accepted, is a theory of the development and working of the mind which was evolved by a Jew who has studied chiefly Jewish patients ; and it seems to appeal very strongly to Jews ; many, perhaps the majority, of those physicians who accept it as a new gospel, a new revelation, are Jews. It looks as though this theory, which to me and to most men of my sort seems so strange, bizarre, and fantastic, may be approximately true of the Jewish race.

Again, one cannot ignore the fact that Jung has a number of ardent disciples who hold his theory true, because they find it helpful in the treatment of their patients. In face of this situation, suspended judgment with an open mind is the only scientific attitude.

But, though in my opinion the evidence adduced by Jung in support of his theory of archetypal ideas is not such as should secure acceptance of the theory by all impartial inquirers, it is worth while to point out that we have no positive knowledge which is incompatible with the theory. It is true that the theory is hardly to be reconciled with the Neo-Darwinian principle which is so widely accepted, somewhat dogmatically, by many biologists at the present time, the principle which denies the possibility of the transmission from generation to generation of the effects of use, the gains of facility and function made by the efforts of each generation. But, as I shall presently insist, this principle is by no means finally established. On the other hand, there is a certain amount of vague evidence, beyond that adduced by Jung, which makes in favour of some such view as his. First, it is becoming generally recognized by biologists that the Darwinian principle of selection is not in itself adequate to account for the evolution of the world of living things, and especially that it is inadequate to account for the evolution of the mental powers of the human species. Secondly, popular opinion, based upon a vast amount of vague and unanalysed experience, is decidedly opposed to scientific opinion in this matter. And in these obscure regions the popular tradition is often more nearly right than the opinion prevailing in the scientific world at any particular phase of the development of science. Scientific opinion is too apt to deny the possibility of alleged forms of happening, on the ground that we cannot understand how such things can happen. It cannot be too strongly insisted that denial on such ground is always unjustified, and that it is especially unjustifiable in the obscure realm of the human mind, about which our positive knowledge is still so scanty and rudimentary. Popular opinion in this matter would seem to be influenced chiefly by similarities in mental traits (both moral traits and peculiar intellectual capacities and tendencies, such as forms of wit, aptitudes for language study, for mechanical contrivance, for imaginative flights) which may often be observed in members of a family. Such similarities may be plausibly attributed to personal contact and imitation in many cases. But in other cases this explanation will not apply; yet the similarities may be very striking. Thirdly, the larger school of psycho-analysts, who follow Freud rather than Jung, find evidence of certain constantly recurring symbols in dreams and fantasies which, if the evidence is sufficiently good, necessitate the assumption of innate factors in the mind very similar to Jung's archetypal ideas.[1] Fourthly, the

[1] I refer more especially to such symbolic images as the snake. In other ways, Professor Freud's own theory of the neuroses implies clearly the principle of inheritance of racial experience, and Professor Freud, in his later writings, has fully recognized this implication. In his " General Introduction to Psycho-analysis " he writes : " I am of the opinion that these *primal phantasies* . . . are a phylogenetic possession. In them the individual reaches out beyond his own life, into the experiences of antiquity. . . . It seems very possible to me that everything which is obtained during an analysis in the guise of phantasy . . . was once realities in the primeval existence of mankind, and that the imaginative child is merely filling in the gaps of individual truth with prehistoric truth."

perennial interest of children in certain kinds of objects (both real and fanciful) of which they have had no experience, but which must have figured much in the imaginations of their remote ancestors, seems to point to the inheritance by the race of some traces of such ancestral experience. It is difficult to account in any other way for the spontaneous and vivid interest of almost all European children in stories of fairies, goblins, ghosts, witches, wolves, bears, caves, and enchanted forests. Fifthly, the development of moral sentiments in many children, their resentment of injustice, their appreciation of honesty and truth-telling, and other such moral reactions, seems so spontaneous and untaught that it is difficult to believe that these moral reactions or moral sentiments are not, in some manner and degree, preformed or hereditary in their constitution. There seem to be large differences between children in respect of the ease with which such moral sentiments develop under the influence of example and training. And if the opinion widely held by alienists and criminologists, to the effect that some children are by nature insusceptible of moral training, though not lacking in intelligence, if this opinion is not utterly baseless, it is strong evidence of the inheritance by the normal child of some preformed moral sentiments, some tendency for such sentiments to take form in the mind spontaneously, however much their development may need to be furthered by experience and moral training. Again, there seem to be national and racial differences in this respect which do not seem to be wholly explicable in terms of differences of national tradition. There are, for example, among both civilized and uncivilized peoples, some which are notoriously untruthful ; some which are remarkably chaste, though not deficient in the sex impulse ; some as remarkably unchaste.

A sixth kind of evidence, pointing in the same vague way to a greater complexity of the innate constitution of the human mind than is commonly recognized by science, is afforded by the testimony of many persons whose work has made them familiar with alien races and with cross-bred races. Thus, it is asserted by many experienced Anglo-Indian officials that education of Hindus by the methods and materials used in European education is positively deleterious to their mental development. And it is widely asserted of some of the populations which have been formed by the blending of widely dissimilar races, that both the intellectual and moral development of the majority of individuals among such populations is seriously defective in some obscure and ill-defined way. It is often alleged that such persons reveal a fundamental lack of harmony in their character, an abnormal liability to moral conflict and disorder.[1]

---

[1] E.g., " It is a common opinion, held by the blacks as well as by the whites, that an infusion of white blood increases the intelligence of the negro, while at the same time lowering his moral qualities." (N. S. Shaler, " The Neighbour.")

NATIONAL WELFARE AND NATIONAL DECAY

I will venture to state tentatively the view to which all these vague lines of evidence seem to me to point. The innate basis of the mind is richer, more complex, than present-day science is willing to admit. On both the moral and the intellectual sides the innate potentialities are richer, more various, and more specific than can be described in terms of degrees of intelligence and degrees of strength of the several instinctive impulses. Just as that peculiarity which enables a man to become a great mathematician (or a great musician) is certainly innate and hereditary, though we cannot define or conceive in what this hereditary basis consists, so also the development of the highest moral character only proceeds upon the basis of a hitherto undefined innate and hereditary peculiarity.

This undefined innate basis of moral character is perhaps of all innate qualities the most valuable possession of any human stock. It is the innate basis of a quality which we may best name trustworthiness. This quality is no simple unit; it cannot be ascribed to the operation of any one instinct; and, though it implies intelligence, it is not closely correlated with high intelligence. In respect of this complex and vaguely defined quality, races and peoples seem to differ widely. Without its presence in a high degree, no people can achieve or sustain a high level of civilization. Consider how the punctual and efficient working of any one of our great public services implies a high degree of trustworthiness on the part of a vast number of persons. When we see a great mail-train glide, punctual to the minute, into the railway terminus after traversing hundreds or thousands of miles of varied territory, after burrowing through mountains, crossing great rivers, winding through deep gorges, thundering across vast plains, we do not often sufficiently realize on how many human beings this achievement has depended, or how great demands on their trustworthiness it has made. It is because such services make these great demands that a people is justly proud of the efficiency, the punctuality, the freedom from accident, and the dependability of such great public services. It is for the same reason that some peoples, even among the civilized nations, seem to be incapable of maintaining efficient services of this kind. It is for this reason that, among many peoples which have established such services, the posts of critical responsibility are generally filled by foreigners, men of a different race which seems to be more highly endowed with this complex quality of trustworthiness. It is not too much to claim for this quality that it is more important than any other, intelligence not excepted, for the maintenance of a high level of civilization. If, in any people that has attained such a high level, this quality should decline (statistically) we might anticipate a corresponding decline in the efficiency of all its public services. We might expect to see its police force become corrupt, its courts of justice less efficient, its criminals bolder and more numerous, its postal deliveries irregular, its railway trains unpunctual and subject to many accidents, its bankruptcies and commercial panics more frequent, its strikes more reckless ; and in war, the supreme test, it would, in spite of much bravery and high intelligence, be relatively ineffective. This is admittedly the expression of a somewhat speculative opinion which cannot claim to be founded on scientifically established facts.

Another speculative question may be touched on here, namely—Is there any correlation between high intelligence and the possession of the more desirable moral qualities ; that is, do these tend to " go together " ; are highly intelligent persons (statistically) on the whole better equipped with · moral qualities than less intelligent persons ? Professor Terman[1] provides some evidence that there is positive correlation between intelligence and the possession of the better moral qualities, and one of considerable degree. If this result is accepted, it does not necessarily follow that the correlation is hereditary ; but it is difficult to account for it in any other way. If such hereditary correlation were established, it would be a fact of · the very first importance ; for the methods of measuring intelligence, which have been proved to be trustworthy by so many extensive researches of recent years, would then provide an indirect measure of the moral qualities, which, though fallible in indi-

[1] " Intelligence of School Children," p. 58.

vidual cases, would be statistically trustworthy.[1]

I mentioned Doctor Jung's theory of archetypes, not only because it serves as a warning against dogmatic negation,[2] but because it raises in an acute form two closely allied questions that are of prime importance for our main topic—namely, the question of the persistence of peculiarities of mental endowment, and the question of the modes and influences by which they undergo change.

Before turning to these topics, let me sum up on the differences of innate mental qualities which seem to be well-founded rather than speculative assumptions. We have seen that the three great races of Europe seem to have possessed distinctive moral qualities, that these are, just like the physical qualities of those races, represented in the modern peoples in various degrees and com-

---

[1] I have found only one other piece of evidence directly supporting Professor Terman's. Mr. H. V. Race (" A Study of a Class of Children of Superior Intelligence," *Journal of Educational Psychology*, 1918), by the aid of mental tests, selected from a large number of children twenty-one who showed the highest degree of intelligence. He then studied these twenty-one children intensively and concluded that " they are apt to be unusually able in various fields of human learning," and " they are highly social in the scientific sense of the term. They tend to have good dispositions and lend themselves generously to the needs of the group."

[2] A warning especially important in view of the fact that some reactionary psychologists are showing a tendency to revert to the old view that the innate basis of the mind comprises nothing more than a number of simple reflex tendencies.

binations, according to the proportions in which they inherit the blood of these three chief races. We have no evidence that these races, or the peoples formed by their partial blendings, differ in degree of intellectual capacity. But, nevertheless, in their highest achievements, in the production of which intellect and character co-operate, we see evidences of qualitative differences in the working of their minds—in art and religion and politics, as we have seen, and I think we may safely add in philosophy and science. In these most purely intellectual spheres, general differences are widely recognized and may be attributed to the same moral peculiarities, subtly influencing and moulding the national traditions of thought. The clearness and perfection of expression of the French and Italians, their preference for logical order and the deductive principle, their formalism, their rationalism—these are traditional national characteristics. They seem to be connected with the impetuousness, the immediacy of expression, and the strong sociability of the Mediterranean race; for these have moulded the languages into instruments of vivid clear-cut logical communication.

The strength of the English intellect is its empiricism, its constant appeal, not to established and clearly formulated principles from which it may deduce conclusions, but rather to new facts. It constantly goes out, like the pioneers so well described by Volney, alone and unconcerned by its loneliness, its detachment from all intellectual

143

precedent and companionship, and looks for new facts and new explanations, without feeling the need of fitting these into the framework of a single logical and consistent system.

The German intellect shows the reflective persistency of the introversion common to its two chief constituent races; in its strong regard for system and organization, in its tendency to accept as true whatever is socially and officially recognized as part of the system of thought, it reveals the submissive and highly sociable tendencies; while it lacks something of the clearness of the Mediterranean and of the pioneering independence and empirical curiosity of the English.

We have found reason to believe that men and races differ in their innate mental constitution, on both the intellectual and the moral sides. Do such peculiarities persist through hundreds, perhaps thousands, of generations? Or is the innate basis of the mind plastic, easily transformed? Can a few generations of intellectual education and moral training appreciably modify or improve the innate constitution of any population?

The answer depends upon an unsolved biological problem, the most urgent of all the biological problems, one which profoundly concerns every State; for many great questions of public policy should be determined largely by the answer to this biological problem, the problem—Are acquired qualities transmitted from one generation to another? The two great English founders of the modern theory of evolution, Darwin and Spencer, believed in such transmission. But at present the majority of biologists deny it. This negation is based upon, deduced from, a theory of a German professor, Weissman, a theory which may or may not be true. Now, one good result of the Great War is that we have broken away from the thraldom to theories of German professors to which the scientific world submitted before the war; and this particular theory is already less confidently held. The theory can be tested and the problem can be solved by intelligently directed experiment.

Such research must occupy some years at least, and in the meantime we have a vast amount of printed matter but no decisive facts to go upon. But from many biological facts we can make this inference with some confidence. Innate qualities are in the main very persistent; and, even if modifications, or qualities acquired by use, are transmitted, the accumulation of such effects is in most, probably all, cases a very slow and gradual process, requiring many generations to produce an appreciable degree of effect.

The persistence of physical qualities is most impressive. We have portraits of Egyptians who lived many thousand years ago, which closely resemble living men of the same region. We have instances of isolated patches of population which, amid all the shiftings and blendings of European peoples, seem to have remained unchanged in physical type for many thousands of years (e.g.

the island of population of the Cro-Magnon type in the Dordogne region of France[1]). We have the curious fact that the blood of various races shows chemical reactions peculiar to each race. As Professor Ripley says : " The persistence of ethnic peculiarities through many generations is beyond question." On the other hand, there are instances in which change of habitat or of mode of life seems to have produced a slowly accumulating change of racial qualities ; for example, life in hill country and life in complex civilized communities—both these seem in the course of many generations to produce somehow a raising of the cephalic index, that is, a relative broadening of the skull.

We must therefore compare branches of the same race which have lived widely apart ; if these remain alike, and if also branches of unlike races which have long lived under similar conditions continue to show in full their racial differences, then we have good evidence of persistence of racial qualities in spite of environmental influences. Such instances are known. The Negro race has long lived in widely separated areas—in Africa, Malaysia, the West Indies, North and South America. Yet it continues to show in all these areas the same fundamental physical qualities and, what is more important, the same mental qualities. And in Malaysia and the Pacific we see populations of Malay and of Polynesian and of Negro blood which have long lived under well-nigh identical

[1] Cf. Ripley's " Races of Europe," p. 179.

conditions, and which nevertheless continue to exhibit in full degree the physical and the mental differences of these races. These facts were pointed out by A. R. Wallace, and I have myself observed them. Some readers may assent easily to the view that physical qualities are very persistent, but may find it difficult to accept the same view of mental qualities. For bones and skulls are solid tangible objects ; they seem durable and persistent. But how can such intangible immaterial entities as mental qualities persist unchanged for thousands of years ? Well, even the qualities of the bony framework are handed down in an utterly mysterious manner, which biologists try to make a little less mysterious by invoking the " continuity of the germ-plasm." And the transmission of mental qualities is no more and no less mysterious than that of physical qualities. But it is well to realize that such mental qualities as the instincts are among the most durable things we know. The great instincts common to most of the higher animals were evolved long before mountain ranges such as the Alps assumed their present form ; and they may well survive when all the mountains that we know shall have been worn away.

Indirect evidence and general considerations point to the great persistence of innate mental qualities, even under changed conditions. The early descriptions of the moral qualities of the inhabitants of Europe, and especially of Gaul, which have come down to us from Tacitus and Cæsar and others, seem to show that the Nordics and the Alpines and the Mediterraneans of that time were distinguished by the same peculiarities which mark them now and which, throughout the historic period, have played their parts in determining the forms of their art, of their customs, and of their institutions.

Even the evidence of Jung and his disciples, which perhaps is the best evidence we have of the gradual modification of innate mental qualities by transmission of the effects of use, is nevertheless at the same time evidence of the strong persistence of such qualities. For the observers of this school claim to be able to trace in living men the influences of customs and ways of thinking which seem to have been impressed on the race thousands of years ago, and which have persisted in spite of all the vicissitudes of the peoples of Europe in the historic period.

Is there any evidence of the opposite kind, pointing to rapid change and plasticity of the racial mental constitution ? It is difficult to find any. One popular fallacy which is commonly accepted as such evidence we may dispose of in a few words. It is often supposed that the superiority of civilized man to his savage forefathers is an innate superiority, which he owes to his long-continued subjection to the influences of culture. It is agreed by those who have considered the matter that there is no good ground for this belief.

The superiority of civilized man consists in, or

arises in the main from, the fact that he has at his command all the accumulated resources and traditions of civilization. There is no good evidence for the belief that he is in any way innately superior to his savage ancestors. In fact, the probability seems to be that he is (statistically) inferior.

CHAPTER VI

WE are now in a position to return a considered answer to the question as to the influence of innate racial qualities upon the course of national life, which was formulated concretely in the second chapter. The question was put in this form. If every infant of one nation were substituted for one of another nation, until the two peoples were completely exchanged, what effects would this substitution have upon their subsequent history? Let us imagine this to have been done in the year 1200 A.D. to the French and British peoples. Obviously, there would have been produced no sudden or violent change of the course of national life in either country. But would there not have taken place a gradual change of customs, laws, and institutions in both countries, so that in many respects they would have approximated to one another; and then perhaps have diverged, after a crossing of their paths? Is it not probable, for example, that France would not only have conquered great areas of the earth, but would have held and peopled them, and that with her more ancient and mature civilization she would have dominated the world ? Is it not probable that the national institutions of France would have gradually acquired a more particularist or individualist form ; and that in England administration would have become more centralized, the family more unified, the laws in general less adapted to give free play to individual initiative ? Is it not probable that the laws of England would have been codified, and those of France left a chaos of precedents, of judicial decisions, of legislative compromises, all unrelated and unharmonized by any clear logical principles or rational system ?

Let me state more generally the view to which all our evidence seems to point. Each people that has attained a high level of civilization has done so on the basis of the intellectual and moral qualities of the races which have entered into its composition. The combination of qualities peculiar to each race was formed and fixed during long ages of the prehistoric period, compared with which the historic period of some 2,500 years is very brief.

These native qualities are the capital, as it were, with which a people sets out on the path of civilization. They are subject to only slow changes ; but they do change, if factors making for change continue to operate in the same direction during many generations. But, like all highly developed qualities of animals and plants, the qualities most necessary for the development and support of civilization are more readily subject to decay or diminution than to further development.

Each people is endowed with qualities which incline it to civilization of a particular type, and which render it capable of supporting a civilization of a given degree of complexity. Each progressive people thus tends to reach the limit of complexity of civilization which is prescribed for it by its innate qualities; when that limit is reached it ceases to progress and is very liable to actual retrogression or decay. For under civilization its qualities tend to deteriorate rather than to improve.

Let us now examine this last statement.

The influences which may produce changes of racial qualities are of three kinds.

(1) Reversion. This is a doubtful factor. It is held by some biologists that any highly developed race will deteriorate, if its qualities are not maintained by continued selection. And it is held that isolation of any race is necessary for the maintenance of its special qualities; for crossbreeding with other races tends to produce reversion to the lower ancestral type. There is some reason to fear that the miscegenation which is going on so widely between human stocks is having this effect; and not only on theoretical grounds. There are some faint empirical indications of it; for example, the northern peoples of Europe are steadily losing their fair complexion—the average complexion is darkening; and, as the fair com-

plexion is undoubtedly a recent specialization, this looks like a case of reversion. Possibly, then, reversion of mental qualities is also going on. But it is possible that this darkening of the complexion of the mixed populations of northern Europe is an effect of a selection which favours the darker strains ; for these seem to be more resistant to the unfavourable influences of town and factory life.

(2) Transmission of acquired qualities, of the effects of use, is a possibility. If it is an actual factor, what must have been its most general effect under civilization ? Which kind of life is more suited to develop to the utmost and, by much exercise, impress more strongly on a population the more valuable qualities—intelligence, independence, initiative, providence, the parental and altruistic tendency, curiosity, and trustworthiness (for these seem to be the most valuable of the fundamental innate qualities) ? Which mode of life, I ask, is more suited to develop these by exercise—that of the hunter, herdsman, warrior, cultivator, living in a well-defined social unit, such as a village community ; or the life of a wage-labourer, a mill-hand, a shop-assistant · or small clerk in one of our highly civilized nations ? There can be no doubt that the advantage is with the former more natural mode of life. We must remember that universal schooling is a recent and but partially achieved ideal, and that schooling is but an imperfect substitute for the education that a boy gets from living vividly the natural

life. This factor, then, probably makes for deterioration, if it is operative at all.

·(3) Selection. It is of the very essence of civilization that, as it progresses, it abolishes more and more completely the operation of the various forms of natural selection which in primitive peoples undoubtedly tend to maintain and promote the racial qualities. And, in our modern western nations, medical science, charitable organization, and protective legislation have pretty well achieved the abolition of natural selection.

Sexual selection may have helped to evolve the higher racial qualities. Under modern conditions, with the prevalence of monogamy and of the excess of females over males, it can hardly be operative. And modern feminism is withdrawing more and more of the best of the women from marriage and motherhood.[1]

Instead of natural and sexual selection, we have operative a number of forms of selection, all of which seem to be injurious to the race.

Military selection involves the death of many of the best and boldest; and it withholds other well-endowed men from early marriage, leaving

---

[1] I have no space to show the facts and inferences, and must refer the reader to an essay by Mr. S. H. Halford on " Dysgenic Tendencies," in the volume on " Population and Birth-Control," edited by C. and E. Paul; New York, 1917. His conclusion is : " In any case there seems no other prospect, if the full feminist ideal be realized, than the entire extinction of British and American intelligence within the next two or three generations " (p. 232).

that privilege to the physically and mentally defective.

Selection by the towns. The towns tend to attract the most vigorous, the most capable and enterprising of the young people of the countryside; in each generation they stream into the towns, leaving an inferior residue in the villages and farms. In New England, as in Old England, the phenomenon is so well known that it is needless to insist on it. But it is not so generally appreciated that the towns not only withdraw the best from the countryside, but destroy these selected strains. For a variety of reasons, the town population does not maintain itself. The great towns are vortices which suck in the best of the population; and, from the racial point of view, they destroy it, for they destroy its natural fertility.

This destructive dysgenic influence of the towns is a part of a wider phenomenon, namely, the operation of the *social ladder* which enables men to pass easily up or down the social scale. In all civilized societies, except those founded upon a rigid caste system, the social ladder exists; and every step forward in democratic organization, everything that throws the world more completely open to talent, that finds the right man for the right place and the square peg for the square hole, educational facilities, scholarships, personnel agencies—all such things contribute to the perfection of the social ladder by which the ascent of merit and the descent of ineptitude are made easy.

Now an effective social ladder in any nation is a most important agency for the advancement of its civilization. In its absence, talent will not find due scope ; the men who, by reason of superior endowments, are its natural leaders will not come to the front. And that such men should be produced by a people and should achieve a due influence upon and leadership in every form of activity, in government, in science, in art, in commerce and industry, is the most essential condition of national prosperity and national progress.[1] Hence the nation with the best social ladder, other things being the same, will for a time progress most rapidly.

The social ladder tends to produce a social stratification ; it tends to a differentiation of society into superimposed strata of unequal value. That this has actually occurred is indicated by the few experimental observations cited (p. 76 *et seq.*) in support of the proposition that degrees of intelligence are hereditary. We need many more such investigations.[2] But the fact is shown by common

[1] This position is argued at some length in my " Group Mind."

[2] Mr. A. W. Kornhauser has recently provided fresh evidence in a paper on " The Economic Standing of Parents and the Intelligence of Their Children " (*Journal of Educational Psychology*, Vol. IX, 1916). He examined 1,000 children, drawn from five schools of the city of Pittsburgh. Of these schools A and B were attended chiefly by the children of the poorer classes, largely unskilled manual workers ; C and D by children of a more prosperous class, largely skilled artisans and small shopkeepers ; E by

observation also ; the process has gone farthest in the country in which the social ladder has been longest in effective operation. Of European countries, England is that country ; hence we find

children of parents of very comfortable circumstances. He found that the groups from A and B " show a very large proportion of Retarded, with an almost negligible number of Advanced " ; C and D groups " have the most nearly normal distribution of Retarded and Advanced " ; the E group " shows the opposite tendency from the first two schools (A and B), namely, a very small proportion of Retarded, with a comparatively large percentage of Advanced pupils. These data in themselves give some indication of the marked association between economic status and school advancement, and undoubtedly would be much more striking if the different schools had a system of uniform grading ; for there can be no question that there is a tendency for the general lower ability in the poor school to be compensated by a general lower standard of grading, and *vice versa* in the wealthier school." That is to say, if the several schools had the same standard of grading, the superiority of intelligence of the children of school E over the others (and of schools C and D over A and B) would be revealed even more strikingly. The same observer obtained a similar result by a different procedure. Taking the possession of a telephone in the home as an indicator of good economic status of the parents, and dividing all the children into the three groups—Retarded, Normal, and Advanced—he found that the following percentages of these three groups had telephones in the home : of the Retarded 19 per cent.; of the Normal 32 per cent.; of the Advanced 50 per cent. These facts afford valuable confirmation of the observations on the correlation of intelligence with social status, set out in the second lecture. For in this case the estimation of the intelligence of the children was made by the school teachers. The terms Retarded and Advanced mean that the child is below or above the school grade in which the average that, as various observers have said, England is a land of great contrasts ; and the top stratum in England, the upper professional and commercial classes, together with the aristocracy, which is constantly recruited from them (and from America), is probably richer in valuable human qualities than any other large human group now existing—or was so before the war ; while the lower strata contain a deplorable proportion of human beings of poor quality.[1] *Se. 165*

That is to say, the operation of the social ladder tends to concentrate the valuable qualities of the whole nation in the upper strata, and to leave the lowest strata depleted of the finer qualities.

This provides the leadership and ability required for the flourishing of national life in all its departments, and in so far is good and beneficial. But the working of the social ladder has further

age is that of the child in question. This question is so important that it seems worth while to add the table showing the percentages of the three classes—Retarded, Normal, and Advanced—in the five schools respectively.

					Retarded.	Normal.	Advanced.
A	.	.	.	.	45·2	47·1	7·7
B	.	.	.	.	36·7	55·9	7·4
C	.	.	.	.	29·4	50·4	20·2
D	.	.	.	.	28·8	51·7	19·5
E	.	.	.	.	12·7	62·7	24·6

[1] *See* Appendix II.

and less satisfactory results. The upper strata,
which contain in concentration the best qualities
of the nation, and which are capable of producing
a far larger proportion of men fitted for leadership
than the lower strata, become relatively infertile.
The causes are varied and complex, and in the
main psychological : late marriage, celibacy, and
restriction of the family after marriage are the
main factors.[1] This is not a new phenomenon or
peculiar to any one or a few countries. It is a
well-nigh universal phenomenon. Roughly, it may
be said to be due to the outstripping of instinct
by intelligence in these favoured classes ; for
instinct cares for the race ; intelligence, save in its
most enlightened forms, for the individual. It is
not confined to the topmost stratum. It begins
there and descends through the strata immediately below. In Britain it has reached the skilled
artisan class, the pick of the wage-earning class,
and is displayed acutely in that class. Mean-
while the lowest strata continue to breed at a
more normal rate ; the birth-rate remains highest
among the actual mental defectives.[2] The residue

[1] Herbert Spencer assumed that there was a natural
physiologically grounded inverse correlation between fertility and intellectual development. It may safely be
said that there is little or no ground for this assumption.
The inverse correlation is well marked, but it is grounded
in psychological rather than physiological factors, and is
therefore subject to rational control and voluntary choice.

[2] The present situation may be roughly described by
saying that the superior half of the population is ceasing
to produce children in sufficient numbers to replace their

in the villages continue to be drained more completely of their best elements ; the towns sift out the best-endowed of these immigrants and pass them up the social scale to become sterilized by their success. The process tends to accelerate and accentuate itself as it continues. Thus, the increasing demands of a civilization of progressing complexity are for a time met by the operation of the social ladder. But it is a process which cannot continue indefinitely. There must come a time when the lower strata, drained of all their best strains, can no longer supply recruits who can effectively fill the gaps in the upper strata and serve as efficient leaders in all the arts and sciences of civilization. With increasing demands and diminishing supply, a point must be reached at which the supply falls short. That is the climax, the culminating point of the parabola of that people ; when a people reaches that point, it stands at the height of its career, but it stands on the brink of the downward plunge of the curve.

It seems to me highly probable that several of the great nations are approaching or have reached that point. I believe that Great Britain has gone farther than any other ; just because the develop-

parents, while the lower half continues to multiply itself freely and is the source of all increase of population. The same statement is probably roughly true of America. The phenomenon is world-wide. As Mr. Halford says (*loc. cit.*) : " The higher races are using the resources of scientific knowledge to reduce the death-rate of the inferior peoples and the birth-rate of the superior."

ment of democratic institutions has proceeded more uninterruptedly and successfully and for a longer time than in any other people ; and also because her stock has been depleted by emigration of vast numbers of persons of more than average vigour and quality. But British complacency refuses to see the signs. In a recent leading article *The Times* solemnly repudiated any such notion, asserting that the nation which in the past has thrown up so much ability, so many great men, will not fail to produce the men needed to meet all future demands.[1] The fatuous belief in the old dictum, that the great occasion or the great need always brings forth the great man to lead the nation over its difficulties, should have been shaken by the Great War. For one of the most striking facts of that prolonged struggle was the failure of the nations involved to bring forth great men adequate to their needs. Did not every nation, France alone excepted, fail to produce a

---

[1] The London *Times*, May 19, 1920. After citing from the report of the registrar-general, which showed clearly the relative infertility of the educated classes, the editorial runs : " We are amused rather than dismayed by the prophets of ' racial suicide ' and have complete confidence in the capacity of the English stock to respond to all the needs of the future." This fatuously complacent utterance was presumably written by a man educated at Oxford, the university whose leading objects of study are history and the writings of Plato, the most thorough-going eugenist of all the social philosophers. And it was written after the Great War, which has done incalculable and irreparable injury to the British stock.

great commander by land or sea ? Did any nation produce a great statesman ? You may say that the problems were harder, the times more difficult, than ever before ; that the inadequacy of men was relative only to the vastness of the needs. Perhaps it was so, though I think not. But, granting this, does not the fact remain an illustration of the law that the demands of civilization tend to outrun the qualities of its bearers ?

During the years of the French revolution and the Napoleonic wars, many soldiers rose from the ranks to become great generals. During the industrial revolution in England, many men rose from the ranks to eminence and high command, men like George Stephenson, and many others of his stamp.

But the social ladder has been at work for several generations since these men rose, and with fatal efficiency. Such rising has become much rarer in the old countries, in spite of the increased encouragement offered in the way of education and rewards.[1] And it is not clear that America is in any better position. It is true that the population is recruited largely by immigration. But these million-a-year immigrants are untested material, they are an uncertain quantity.[2] In the old days men and women did not emigrate to America, unless

[1] This fact is brought out by Mr. Havelock Ellis's " Study of British Genius."

[2] I remind the reader that two observers have found the children of Italian immigrants to be decidedly lower in the scale of intellectual capacity than those of the older white population.

they were persons of more than average vigour, initiative, enterprise, and independence. But the steamship companies, and the spread of civilization and of immigrants from all parts of the world,

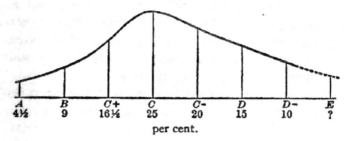

A	B	C+	C	C-	D	D-	E
4½	9	16½	25	20	15	10	?

per cent.

The curve of distribution of intelligence in the young manhood of the American people, as revealed by army tests, runs as in the figure.

have altered all that. And in America the social ladder works with great efficiency ; while the rule of the infertility of the selected classes seems to be rigidly maintained.[1]

[1] And the old stock is dying out. Mr. L. Quessel reviews the evidence of " Race Suicide in the United States " in an essay in the volume on " Population and Birth-Control " (edited by C. and E. Paul) and concludes : " All available data combine to prove that the Anglo-American population has not merely attained its maximum, but has already begun to decline." He adds : " It is perfectly clear that the low birth-rate among the Anglo-American population is not the result of natural sterility, but is due to a deliberate restriction of births."

In this all-important matter of birth-control the position of America is remarkable and uniquely disastrous. The educated classes seem to cultivate and practise the principles of birth-control more assiduously than any other

The educated classes of New England cannot maintain the fatuous complacency of the editor of the London *Times* ! For they have first-hand knowledge of old and formerly valuable populations, now drained of all that was best and reduced to stagnation. They exemplify in the highest degree the rule of the infertility of the selected classes. They have first-hand acquaintance with the process of substitution of population of one type by another, and with the consequent social effects. For them these things are not vague and fanciful possibilities ; they are actual.

Let us recall to mind the curve of distribution of intelligence. Intelligence, as I said, is only one of many factors ; but it is one of considerable importance.

In Great Britain there has been no attempt at a mental survey of the population. It is probable that if such a survey were made, it would reveal a state of affairs very similar to that which obtains in America, as shown by the application of mental tests to an immense number of recruits for the army. In the rating used in reporting the results of this testing, A men are of the grade which " has the ability to make a superior record in college " ; B men are " capable

class of persons of the civilized world, while, *mirabile dictu*, they maintain laws which forbid the extension of the knowledge of such principles to the mass of the people. Doctor M. S. Iseman has drawn a lurid picture of this state of affairs in his " Race Suicide " (New York, 1912).

of making an average record in college"; C men are "rarely capable of finishing a high-school course." The main bulk of the population is below the C + level.[1]

[1] That is to say, the results of the army tests indicate that about 75 per cent. of the population has not sufficient innate capacity for intellectual development to enable it to complete the usual high-school course. The very extensive testing of school-children carried on by Professor Terman and his colleagues leads to closely concordant results. He divides the children on the basis of his tests into the following classes (and it should be added that the school-status of the children and the judgments of their teachers bear out the grading very fully) : Border-line cases (scoring 70–80 marks in the testing). These roughly correspond to the groups D —and E of the army tests, and are about 8 per cent. of the whole number of school-children. Of these Professor Terman says . "According to the classical definition of feeble-mindedness, such individuals cannot be considered defectives. Hardly anyone would think of them as institutional cases. Among labouring men and servant girls there are thousands like them. They are the world's hewers of wood and drawers of water. And yet, as far as intelligence is concerned, the tests have told the truth These boys are uneducable beyond the merest rudiments of training. No amount of school instruction will ever make them intelligent voters or capable citizens in the true sense of the word. . . . It is interesting to note that [children of this grade] represent the level of intelligence which is very, very common among Spanish-Indian and Mexican families of the South-west and also among Negroes. Their dullness seems to be racial, or at least inherent in the family stocks from which they come The fact that one meets this type with such extraordinary frequency among Indians, Mexicans, and Negroes suggests quite forcibly that the whole question of racial differences in mental traits will have to be taken up anew, and by experimental methods " Above these comes

165

The civilization of any country depends on its continuing to produce in fair numbers men of the calibre of the A and B classes. At present the A men are 4½ per cent., the B men 9 per cent., in America ; and in Britain they may be a little more or less numerous proportionately ; the difference in either direction can hardly be more than 2 or 3 per cent. ; and we are breeding from the lower part of the curve. The A men and B men do not maintain their numbers ; while the population continues to grow.[1] If this goes on for a few

the group of " dull normals " (scoring 80–90 marks). They constitute about 15 per cent. of the whole number and correspond roughly to the D group of the army tests—" they are far enough below the actual average of intelligence among races of western European descent that they cannot make ordinary school progress." The third group is of " average intelligence " (scoring 90–110 marks) and comprises about 60 per cent. of the whole number. " The high school does not fit their grade of intelligence as well as the elementary and grammar schools." They correspond roughly to the groups C —, C, and the lower part of C + of the army tests. Next comes the group of " superior intelligence " (scoring 110–120 marks). It comprises about 15 per cent. of the whole, and corresponds to the upper part of group C + and to groups B and A of the army tests.

[1] Harvard graduates, it is said, have less than two children apiece on the average, and the same is probably true approximately of the graduates in general. With the graduates of women's colleges the case seems to be still worse. Professor J. McK. Cattell asserts : " Among the educated and well-to-do classes the number of children does not nearly suffice to continue the race. The Harvard graduate has on the average seven-tenths of a son, the Vassar graduate one-half of a daughter " (Popular Science

generations, will not the A men, and even the B men, become rare as white elephants, dropping to a mere fraction of one per cent. ? It is only too probable.

The present tendency seems to be for the whole

Monthly, January, 1909). For a full revelation of the facts in regard to college women, see Popenoe and John-son's " Applied Eugenics," chap. XII. Professor Karl Pearson has shown that the most prolific sixth (or less) of the population in Great Britain produces 50 per cent. of the children of each generation. It is in the highest degree probable that this one-sixth belongs almost wholly to the . right or inferior end of the curve.

Professor Pearson wrote : " The upper middle classes are the result of a severe selection of capacity, and, later, of intermarrying, under conditions which seem no longer possible." . . . " It is the realization of these points, that not all, but the bulk, of the abler and more capable stocks have drifted into the upper middle classes, and that ability is inherited,which makes, in my opinion, the decreasing relative fertility of these classes a matter of the most serious national importance " ('' National Life from the Standpoint of Science," London, 1905).

In view of the heavy burdens imposed by the war on the professional classes in Britain, it is only too probable that the state of affairs which Professor Pearson deplored in 1905 has become very much worse.

In an article in the volume " Heredity and Eugenic " (Chicago, 1913), Doctor C. B Davenport, one of the highest authorities on these matters, gives us the following interest-ing calculation. Writing of the graduates of Harvard ʾCollege, he states : " At the present rate [of reproduction] 1,000 graduates of to-day will have only 50 descendants 200 years hence. On the other hand, recent immigrants and the less effective descendants of the earlier immigrants still continue to have large families, so that from 1,000 Roumanians to-day in Boston, at the present rate of breeding, will come 100,000 " after the same space of time, namely, 200 years. Blind optimists, confronted with the curve to shift to the right with each successive generation.[1] And this is probably true of moral qualities, as well as of intellectual stature. If the time should come when our A and B men together are no more than one per cent., or a mere fraction of one per cent., of the population—what will become of our civilization ?

facts of the dying out of the old American stocks, are apt to remark that the rate of reproduction of the new immigrants will also decline. This is probably true of those among them who have the moral and intellectual capacity to climb the social ladder ; but that is not a consoling reflection. Substitute for the 1,000 Roumanians of the foregoing calculation 1,000 mental defectives (and these are only a small fraction of the total number in the Boston area) and you have a more exact picture of the present tendency of change in the population. For the mental defectives are, it appears, the most persistently prolific class of the population, so long as they are left at liberty to do as they please.

[1] Since it has been shown that actual mental defectives are the most prolific part of the population, it is of some interest to estimate their numbers. Authorities give various estimates ; for the class is not yet defined in any generally accepted manner. Most authorities seem to estimate them as above 2 per cent. of the population in America. Goddard, the highest authority in the matter, says : " It is a conservative estimate to declare that 2 per cent. of public-school children are distinctly feeble-minded ; . . . the most extensive study . . . of an entire school system of 2,000 has shown that 2 per cent. of such children are so mentally defective as to preclude any possibility of their ever being made normal and able to take care of themselves as adults." Others have estimated the feeble-minded in the schools as high as 4 per cent. To these have to be added the declared defectives who are not sent to the public schools.

Let me state the case more concretely, in relation to one of the great essential professions of which I have some inside knowledge, namely, the medical profession. Two hundred or one hundred years ago, the knowledge to be acquired by the medical student, before entering upon the practice of his profession, was a comparatively small body of empirical rules. The advance of civilization has enormously multiplied this knowledge; and the very existence of our civilized communities depends upon the continued and effective application of this vast body of medical art and science. The acquiring and the judicious application of this mass of knowledge make very much greater demands upon the would-be practitioner than did the mastery of the body of rules of our forefathers. Accordingly, the length of the curriculum prescribed for our medical students has constantly been drawn out, till now its duration is some six years of postgraduate study.

The students who enter upon this long and severe course of study are already a selected body; they have passed through school and college successfully. We may fairly assume that the great majority of them correspond to the A or B men in the scale of intelligence applied to the American army.[1]

What proportion of them prove capable of assimilating the vast body of medical knowledge to the point that renders them capable of applying

[1] Or to Professor Terman's groups of superior and very superior intelligence.

it intelligently and effectively ?   If I may venture to generalize from my own experience, I would say that a very considerable proportion, even of those who pass their examinations, fail to achieve such effective assimilation.   The bulk of modern medical knowledge is too vast for their capacity of assimilation, its complexity too great for their power of understanding.   Yet medical science continues to grow in bulk and complexity, and the dependence of the community upon it becomes ever more intimate ;   for the natural resistance of the population to disease declines, in proportion as the population is effectively protected by medical science from the selective action of diseases.

In this one profession, then, which makes such great and increasing demands on both the intellectual and the moral qualities of its members, the demand for A and B men steadily increases ; and the supply in all probability is steadily diminishing with each generation.

And what is taking place in this one profession is, it would seem, taking place in all the great professions and higher callings. *Our civilization, by reason of its increasing complexity, is making constantly increasing demands upon the qualities of its bearers ; the qualities of those bearers are diminishing or deteriorating, rather than improving.*

If we turn now to consider very briefly the history of the great peoples of the past, we find evidence which bears out my main thesis, which goes far to substantiate the explanation of the Parabola of Peoples suggested in these pages.

The most glorious civilization of the past was that of ancient Greece. We do not know the ethnic composition of the people which produced that civilization. It is still a matter of dispute.[1] But we do know that the present population of Greece is in the main of different stock.[2] And history shows that the change or substitution of population took place about the time of the decay of that civilization. The causes of this disaster were many. There was the psychological infertility of the selected classes, with the decay of marriage and family life. There was exile and colonization, both on a great scale ; and there was almost perpetual warfare, largely of Greek against Greek ; all tending strongly to the elimination of the most fit. There was finally, and on a great scale, exportation of Greeks by their Roman conquerors, as slaves to do the clerical and professional work of the Roman Empire. No wonder that the collapse of that civilization, borne by so small a population, was sudden and complete !

The grandeur that was Rome endured for a

[1] It has been maintained by many that it was predominantly Nordic. The most probable view seems to be that, like the English, the population of ancient Greece was, in the main, a mixture and partial blend of the Nordic and Mediterranean races, enriched by the attraction of many choice individuals from surrounding countries.

[2] Ripley ("Races of Europe," p. 407) shows that, whereas the ancient Greeks were (statistically) long-headed, the modern population is predominantly short-headed, presumably owing to the predominance of Slavic blood.

longer space; for it was founded upon a broader basis of population. During some centuries the Roman Empire drew into its service the best energies and talents of all the populations of Europe. Common soldiers from remote provinces rose to be emperors or governors; slaves imported from afar became secretaries of state and skilled administrators. The whole Empire was one great vortex, sweeping to its centre the best talents of the civilized world. All roads led toward Rome. And the rule of the infertility of the selected classes prevailed. Marriage became unfashionable, children were regarded as a burden. Pleasure, luxury, and the production of elegant Latin verse became the leading preoccupations of the selected classes. The Church, with her advocacy of celibacy and her doctrine that it is better to marry than to burn, lent her powerful aid. For many generations the process went on, the process of the extermination of the most valuable strains; in Otto Seeck's expressive phrase, the process of the " Ausrottung der Besten."[1] The mistress of the world reached the climax of her parabola and rapidly declined; and the chaos of the early middle ages succeeded.

The next great empire comparable to Rome's was that of Spain—a wonderful and brilliant career, but of short duration. The expulsion of the Moors and of the Jews, the work of the Inquisition, the

[1] " Geschichte des Untergangs der Antiken Welt." See also Professor J. L. Myres, " Changes of Population in the Classical World," *Eugenic Review*, 1917.

celibacy of the Church, perpetual warfare, the drain of a vast colonial empire, and the luxury and wealth derived from it—all these combined to sap away the strains of finest quality; and the power and glory of Spain rapidly declined. France and England took up the struggle and fought for the mastery of the world.

Germany, coming relatively late under the devastating influences of our industrial civilization, has made her bid for world domination and has failed; and, incidentally, has left the battle-fields of Europe and the Near East strewn with the corpses of.the best and bravest of our young men : brilliant young poets and scientists, inventors and authors and administrators, by the score and by the hundred are lying there, without descendants to perpetuate their talents, leaving the world for ever poorer and the peoples of Europe diminished in moral and intellectual stature for all time.

Westward the march of empire takes its way, throwing out before it a vanguard of pioneers, of the best and brightest and most vigorous. Already the centre of gravity, of power, has passed by the Eastern States of America. The Middle West is already claiming predominance; and the day of the Far West is at hand. And after that—what ?

The process has acquired a frightful rapidity and momentum. Every feature of American civilization seems to conspire for its acceleration, for the more rapid attainment of the climax of the curve and the subsequent decline, and in Great Britain the war, directly by its slaughter and indirectly by the burdens of taxation and the destruction of the patrimonies of many families of the professional classes, must have done more injury to the national stock than many years of peace.

One factor alone can secure our future and save us as a people from the fatal decline, and may even secure for us a continued progress in all that makes the worth of human living.

It is the increasing knowledge of human nature and of human society, and of the conditions that make for or against the flourishing of human nature and society. But the mere increase of such knowledge in scientific academies is of no avail, if that knowledge is not widely diffused among the people, and if it does not become a guide to action in public and in private life.

Fortunately, there is widley diffused a belief in the value of science and of its application to human life. Many keen workers are adding to the sum of knowledge, and we are learning to be guided by it. Therein lies our hope for the future. Such knowledge is virtually a new factor in history. And the essential problem before us is—Can we so make use of this new factor, this increasing knowledge of human nature and human society as to turn the course of history? Can we by taking thought, and action guided by thought, prevent or indefinitely postpone that decline of the curve of civilization which seems even now to threaten us ? What steps we should take ; what changes of law, of social organization, of domestic institutions, we shall, upon mature consideration, institute, I do not suggest. To make any such suggestions is no part of my task in this short study. It is enough if I have directed attention to this supremely important problem ; if I have led my readers to see that every wide measure of social legislation, every custom and social institution, should be judged and evaluated with reference to its bearing upon this problem—its probable effect on the anthropologic constitution of the nation and the sum of its human qualities. All such laws and customs and institutions have their inevitable effects of this all-important kind. The laws regulating the sale of alcohol ; the immigration laws ; the laws of marriage and divorce ; the educational system ; the relations of labour to capital ; the nature and degree of state-interference with personal liberty ; the distribution of the population in town and village ; the size and type of the cities—all these are but a few instances of influences capable of exerting subtle but profound effects upon the quality of the population of the modern State.

But most important of all is the diffusion of the sense of individual responsibility in this matter ; the clear realization that, in the last resort, the future will be the creation of the present, that the nation of the future must issue from the individual choice and action of those who now compose it.

APPENDIX I

COMMENTARY ON THE PROPOSITION THAT ALL MEN ARE
BORN WITH EQUAL CAPACITIES FOR MORAL AND
INTELLECTUAL DEVELOPMENT

PORTRAITS OF THREE MEN, ALL OF WHOM IN
THEIR YOUTH WERE DENIED THE
ADVANTAGES OF SCHOOLING AND THE
REFINEMENTS OF CIVILIZATION

12

This man, by virtue of his qualities of character and intellect, rose from a very humble station to a position of the highest responsibility and power. He so filled that position as to gain the unbounded admiration of all men and of all nations.

APPENDIX I

This man, my friend Tama Bulan, was the chief of a small village in the heart of Borneo. He and his people belonged to one of the tribes which have often been described as degraded savages, stigmatized as head-hunters, and erroneously stated to be cannibals. By reason of his high intelligence, his humane feeling, his firmness of character and statesmanlike foresight, he acquired a great moral influence not only over the people of his own village and tribe, but over many of the other tribes throughout a large area. He used this influence to bring to an end the chronic tribal warfare which in all that region of the earth had long prevailed. By his influence and example he brought peace, happiness, and prosperity to many thousands of his fellow men. Some account of him and his people may be found in " The Pagan Tribes of Borneo," by Charles Hose and William. McDougall (London, 1912).

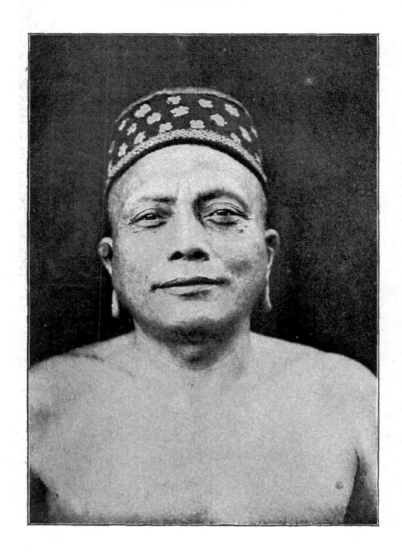

This man remained unknown to fame, until he was photographed by the authors of a recently published book [1] as a representative specimen of the inferior type of the Ila-speaking people.

We are told nothing of his moral and intellectual qualities ; but the most resolutely optimistic humanitarians will hardly claim him as a " mute inglorious Milton," or even as a " village Hampden." Nor is it easy to suppose that they could contemplate with equanimity the substitution of the Anglo-American stock by persons of this type.

[1] " The Ila-speaking People of Northern Rhodesia," by Rev. E. W. Smith and Captain A. M. Dale, London, 1920. I am indebted to Mr. Smith for the copy of the picture.

APPENDIX I

183

APPENDIX II

Birth Rate in the Social Strata

IN Great Britain little has been done in the way of anthropometric survey by the methods of mental measurement. But there has recently been published a survey, by the method of personal interview and estimation, of a large sample of the " manual workers " of Sheffield (" The Equipment of the Workers," London, 1919). Sheffield is a typical manufacturing town of some half-million inhabitants, seated in Yorkshire, near the border of Lancashire ; these two counties are noted for the vigour and achievement of many of their sons and daughters. The investigation dealt with 866 men and women in equal numbers. They were divided into three classes : A, the well-equipped ; B, the inadequately equipped ; C, the mal-equipped. Class A consists of men and women who, as judged by personal impression, by their mode of life and history, seem to be of character (often of fine character) and abilities such as enable them to cope with the problems of life in a satisfactory manner. Their personalities and life-histories may be contemplated with satisfaction, entire sympathy, and considerable admiration. If these were a fair sample of the " manual workers " of the whole country, Britain would be, indeed, a great and happy land. But, unfortunately, they constitute less than one-fourth of the whole group (about 22 per cent.).

13   185

Class C constitutes one-fourteenth of the whole. They are a bad lot. " In stupidity or in ignorance or in base cleverness, those in this class live for ends of their own, in vicious ways that pollute the lives of others. From their loins came the intellectually feeble and the morally depraved children that sap all the best energies of the school-mistress."

Class B comprises all who fall between the levels of classes A and C. " These, in their scores of thousands in Sheffield, and in their millions upon millions in the whole country, are the real ' masses,' the real ' poor,' the real ' people.' . . . They manage to live their own lives and to keep quite as free as the average member of the well-to-do classes from vice and crime. What distinguishes them, or ' indistinguishes ' them, so to speak, is their lack of positive qualities of any kind. . . . It is our honest belief that neither the man, nor—still more certainly—the woman, in Class II (i.e., B) can in any genuine sense of the word be called ' fit to vote.' " They form 70 per cent. of the " manual workers." Detailed notes on a score of individuals from each of the classes A and B are given, these being regarded as fair samples of the two classes. A careful comparison of the detailed descriptions of these samples from the two classes points, I think, clearly to the conclusion that the difference between Classes A and B is in the main one of intrinsic or innate quality and cannot be ascribed to differences of training or educational opportunity. None of Class A (with one doubtful exception) had attended school beyond the fourteenth year ; several of them are described as illiterate, or ignorant, or " never reads," or " scarcely any education." The average of schooling and home training is not appreciably less in Class B. Yet one is made to feel that the average " civic worth " of Class A is vastly greater than that of Class B. The authors of the volume imply (probably correctly) that the majority of the members of Class B might have been made into fairly satisfactory citizens, even made " fit to vote," if the social and educational conditions under which they grew up had been very much better than they actually were, if each one had been carefully trained and fully educated in a good school and home and shielded from all degrading influences. But the striking fact remains that, of the " manual workers " of this representative group, nearly one-quarter grew to be good citizens, in spite of many adverse circumstances, while three-quarters of them failed so to grow. Would it not make a vast difference to the future of Britain, to the welfare and happiness of the whole population, and to the political stability, wisdom, and beneficent world-influence of the country, if the next generation of "manual workers" could come wholly from the loins of Class A. As the writers point out, the elimination of the relatively small Class C would bring the country in sight of Utopia. But other investigators have made it appear only too probable that Class C is the most prolific, and Class A the least prolific, of the three classes. Thus it has been shown that the birth-rate among members of the Hearts of Oak Benefit Society, fell below 15 per 1,000, while that of the population at large remained a little above 30 per 1,000 (Chapple's " Fertility of the Unfit "). Now the members of the Hearts of Oak Society are in the main the pick of the " manual workers," just such persons as make up the Class A of the Sheffield " manual workers."

A strong inverse correlation of the birth-rate with social status seems to be general throughout the European nations. The proof of it in Great Britain and in the United States of America is overwhelmingly strong. Karl Pearson and his associates have proved it for London beyond question ; especially David Heron (" On the Relation of Fertility in Men to Social

Status," London, 1906) and Newsholme and Stevenson (" The Decline of Human Fertility," London, 1906). The last-named authors sum up by saying : " The figures show in a manner which hardly admits of any doubt that in London at any rate the inhabitants of the poorest quarters—over a million in number—are reproducing themselves at a much greater rate than the more well-to-do." A similar state of affairs was shown to obtain before the war in Holland, in Berlin, and in Vienna. In America the evidence is not so complete. But similar facts have been demonstrated for Pittsburgh. In that city " Ward 7 has the lowest birth-rate and the lowest rate of net increase of any ward in the city. With this may be contrasted the Sixth Ward. . . . Nearly 3,000 of its 14,817 males of voting age are illiterate. Its death-rate is the highest in the city. Almost nine-tenths of its residents are either foreigners or the children of foreigners. Its *birth-rate is three times that of the Seventh Ward*. Taking into account all the wards of the city, it is found that the birth-rate *rises* as one considers the wards which are marked by a large foreign population, illiteracy, poverty, and a high death-rate. . . . The correlation between illiteracy and net increase is $+ .731$. The net increase of Pittsburgh's population, therefore, is greatest where the percentage of foreign-born and of illiterates is greatest. . . . Pittsburgh, like probably all large cities in civilized countries, breeds from the bottom. The lower a class is in the scale of intelligence, the greater is its reproductive contribution." (P. Popenoe and R. H. Johnson, " Applied Eugenics," New York, 1918, p. 138.)

The fact of the greater rate of increase of the poorer classes (or, more generally, the inverse correlation of fertility with good social status) is abundantly established ; it cannot be denied by our resolute optimists and fatuously complacent editors. When these people condescend to consider this fact, they usually take the line that " one man is as good as another, and sometimes a good deal better, too." They deny that there is any correlation between position in the social scale and intrinsic or native worth. It may be hoped that the facts of correlation of intelligence with social status, recited in the pages of this book, may lead such persons to consider the problem more seriously. But we need more evidence on the point.[1] It is much to

[1] The last resort of those who are unwilling to accept the evidence of positive correlation between intelligence and good social status is to assert that the children of the better social classes are stimulated to more rapid intellectual development in their earliest years by contact with their more intellectual parents. This explanation has been fully considered and rejected by the workers who have obtained the evidence. I will merely point out here how little ground there is for this assumption. The children of the better social classes, especially perhaps in England, too often spend most of the waking hours of their early years shut away in a nursery, with little or no companionship beyond that of a dull nursemaid, or sitting solemnly in a baby-cart which is pushed round and round some public park. The children of the poor enjoy in the main far more companionship, both childish and adult, have more stimulating contacts, are thrown more upon their own resources, and are much less inhibited and repressed. In consequence, they are notoriously precocious and sharp-witted in their early years ; the London gamin is celebrated in this respect. The life of the street and the gutter may have many dangers, moral and physical, but it is at least stimulating. As Mrs. Dewey, a high educational authority, says in a recent article : " Not the least advantage of being born poor is the opportunity it offers for getting real experience in childhood " (*The Nation*, No. 2913). Perhaps no one but a parent who has lived intimately with his children, striving day by day and night by night to promote their development, can fully realize how refractory is the natural process of unfolding to all our efforts.

be regretted that the Sheffield investigators seem to have paid no attention to the question of the birth-rate among their three classes. Children are mentioned, but the number is not stated in most cases—an illustration of the blindness to this all-important topic of so many earnest social workers.

Some years ago I made a rough census of the families of such of the married resident teachers of Oxford as were known to me and my collaborators. This group included 142 members of this highly intellectual selected class and may fairly be regarded as a true sample. I found that each of these 142 men had on the average 1.8 children ; that is to say, 284 adults (142 married couples) had 261 children. A few of these couples, being still comparatively young, would produce more children ; but of the then existing children some would die before becoming adults. These two unknown quantities are probably not very unequal. In estimating the reproduction rate of this highly selected class, we must take into the account the fact of the very large number of bachelors within it, who, being well advanced in years, are not likely to marry. It was easy to count 70 elderly bachelors, all men of intellectual distinction.

APPENDIX III

The New Plan

WHAT is to be done about it? That is the urgent question in the mind of every serious man or woman who understands the facts and is not utterly blind to the teachings of history. Many social philosophers from Plato onward have advocated measures for the preservation or improvement of racial qualities. Some of these, including Plato's stud-stable method and the practices of infanticide and abortion, which were common among the Spartans and other Greeks, cannot be approved or legally recognized to-day without grave danger of deterioration of our common morality, without loss of much of that improvement of the moral tradition which European civilization has undoubtedly achieved in the last two thousand years, and which we owe so largely to the teachings of the Founder of Christianity. Yet much can be done. Our aim in general must be to favour increase of the birth-rate among the intrinsically better part of the population and its decrease among the inferior part. The first essentials are the further acquisition of knowledge of the facts and principles involved, a wide diffusion of such knowledge, and the building up of a strong public opinion. The second and third are now more important than the first; for, though more exact knowledge is desirable, we have sufficient to serve for sure general guidance.[1]

[1] Messrs. Popenoe and Johnson say: "The basal difference in the mental traits of man (and the physical as

191

The firm and sufficient basis of the demand for eugenic measures is the long-recognized fact that you may not expect to gather figs from thistles or grapes from thorns. More explicitly it may be stated as follows : Human qualities, both mental and physical, are hereditary ; and any human stock is capable of being improved by training and education, by good environmental influences, very slowly only, if at all, and probably not at all. Human beings, far from being born with equal potentialities of moral and intellectual development, inherit these in very different degrees. Any population may in principle be regarded as consisting of two halves ; the half made up of all individuals the sum of whose innate qualities or potentialities is above the average or mean value, and the other half made up of individuals the sum of whose qualities is below the mean value. If these two halves have persistently unequal birth-rates (and the difference of birth-rates is not compensated by an equal difference in their death-rates), that population will undergo a change of quality ; and a small difference of birth-rate is capable of producing a surprisingly large change of quality in the course of a few generations. We have overwhelmingly strong grounds for believing that in this country (and in almost all the countries

well, of course) are known to be due to heredity, and little modified by training. It is therefore possible to raise the level of the human race—the task of eugenics—by getting that half of the race which is, on the whole, superior in the traits that make for human progress and happiness, to contribute a larger proportion to the next generation than does the half which is on the whole inferior in that respect. Eugenics need know nothing more, and the smoke of controversy over the exact way in which some trait or other is inherited must not be allowed for an instant to obscure the known act that the level can be raised." (*Op.* cit., p. 114.)

192

APPENDIX III

of Western civilization) the birth-rate of the inferior
half of the population is very considerably greater
than that of the superior half ; and this greater birth-
rate is only very partially compensated by a higher
death-rate. The problem of eugenics is to equalize the
birth-rate of the two halves (while all efforts to reduce
to a minimum the death-rate of both halves are continued) or, if possible, to reverse the prevailing tendency
and to secure, in the superior half of the population,
a higher birth-rate than that of the inferior half. If
the present state of affairs shall continue, our civilization is doomed to rapid decay. If equalization of the
birth-rate of the two halves can be brought about, the
country may face the future with some hope of continued
prosperity. If the present tendency can be reversed,
and the birth-rate of the superior half be maintained
at a higher rate than that of the inferior half, then, even
though the difference be but slight, we may face the
future with a well-grounded hope that we are building
up the most glorious civilization that the world has
ever seen, the reign of justice, freedom, and kindness
throughout every land.

The knowledge we have amply justifies the eugenic
demand ; the facts are becoming, and will become,
more and more widely appreciated ; a strong public
opinion is being created. But, given the diffusion of
such knowledge and such public opinion, how shall
they be applied to secure the desired effects ? It is
now generally agreed that the reproduction of the
least fit, especially of those persons who are indis-
putably feeble-minded, should be prevented. Public
opinion is already aroused on this matter ; some steps
have been taken, and others will follow. There is
good ground for hope that within a few decades we shall
effectively deal with this most immediately urgent
evil, the high birth-rate of the admittedly and grossly
unfit. It is needless to argue here the relative advantages

of sterilization and of institutional segregation. Probably both methods will be used.

But such measures, though they will immediately obviate a large amount of human suffering and will effect a great public economy, will postpone only a little the deterioration of quality which threatens the whole nation with decay. Some writers on this topic (e.g., Professor Knight Dunlap in his " Personal Beauty and Race Betterment ") have expressed the hope that the wider diffusion of knowledge of methods of birth-control (the contra-ceptive methods) will have a very beneficial effect. Up to the present, such knowledge, diffusing itself downward through the social strata, seems to have diminished very markedly the reproduction of that part of the population (amounting perhaps nearly to one-half of it) which is above the average (statistically) in native qualities ; so that its effects hitherto have been gravely dysgenic or racially detrimental. Further diffusion may partially rectify this dysgenic influence ; but it seems highly improbable that it can, of itself, even completely neutralize it ; it is still more improbable that such knowledge will ever operate as a positively eugenic influence.

Professor Dunlap is optimistic enough to suppose that the further diffusion of this knowledge will solve the " Negro problem " of America. It is to be feared that it will have, among the coloured people, only the positively dysgenic effects which it already produces on so great a scale in the white population ; that among both white and coloured people it will be put into practice only by the more far-sighted, prudent, and self-controlled ; while the most ignorant, careless, and improvident will continue to behave as they always have behaved.

Something may be hoped from the influence upon individual conduct of an enlightened public opinion and sentiment. But, again, it seems highly improbable that this factor alone, or in conjunction with the one last considered, will ever suffice to reverse or even to arrest the process of deterioration.[1] There can be little doubt that the economic factor is of dominant importance in determining the rate of reproduction in all classes but the very poorest and the very richest. The outstanding fact of our present civilization is that the vast majority of men and women are striving to rise, or to maintain themselves, in the social and economic scale, and that the addition of each child to a family is a very serious handicap, a great additional weight, to be borne by the parents who are engaged in this struggle. The acute realization of this fact is the principal ground of the restriction of the birth-rate in recent times among those who have succeeded in rising above the lower social levels. If this be admitted, and I do not think it is seriously questioned by anyone who is competent to form an opinion in the matter, it follows that we must look to some re-adjustment of family incomes as the chief eugenic measure of the future. It may be remarked that no general raising of the level of prosperity and of the standard of living is likely to have the desired effect in any appreciable degree. For the demands of men (and of women) for the good things which money can secure are practically unlimited; and the demands or desires for such things of any particular family are, in the main, relative to the standard set by their social equals, by the social circle to which by occupation and education they belong. This standard of demand at any social level is the product of the interplay of many factors, and, though it undergoes absolute and relative changes, it is fairly stable. In the main it corresponds to the purchasing power of the remuneration com-

[1] It is notorious that the crusade of President Roosevelt and of many other eminent men against " race suicide " in America seems to have had no appreciable effect.

monly received by persons of the average education and abilities of the class concerned ; and this remuneration tends in the main to be such as will permit the satisfaction of the standard demands of a family of three or four persons, that is, a family containing one or two children. Each addition to the family, beyond this minimum number, entails an inability to attain the satisfaction of the standard demands of the class to which it belongs, entails the going without some one or more of the good things of life which other families of similar social level enjoy—it may be domestic service, a piano, a motor-car, college education for the children, foreign travel, a country house, etc., etc. Nor would an absolute equality of income for all families and classes meet the case. If that state of affairs could be maintained, it is clear, I think, that its effects would be positively dysgenic in a high degree. It is equally clear that the general indiscriminating State endowment of motherhood, now called for in so many quarters, would have directly dysgenic effects ; and it would be disastrous, in that it would go very far to destroy the family as an institution of any nation which should adopt this plan. All such schemes should be condemned on the general and sufficient ground that the national welfare and social justice demand that each worker should be remunerated in proportion to the value of the services that he renders to the community. For only in this way are men effectively stimulated to put forth their best efforts and to prepare themselves and their children to render the more valuable and more arduous and (what is in the main the same thing) the more intellectual forms of service.

What is required to counteract the very powerful dysgenic influence of the economic consideration, or prudence, is that every family which has risen above the mean social level (or, better still perhaps, every family which has any good claim to belong to what

APPENDIX III

may be called "the selected classes") should know
that the addition of each child should automatically
bring with it an increase of income sufficient to meet
the expenses normally incurred in the bringing-up
of that child. It is clear that, in order to meet this
requirement, the amount of increase of income would
have to bear some given proportion to the income already
enjoyed or earned. This increase of income should,
I suggest be not less than one-tenth of the earned
income and might well be rather more. A family
earning an income of £500 a year would then receive,
for each living child under the age of, say, twenty years,
an additional income of £50 a year. If such increase
of income, proportional to the earnings and to the
number of children, could be secured to each family
of the selected classes, the eugenic effect would, I submit,
be very great, far surpassing in this direction the effect
of any other eugenic measure that has been proposed ;
while it would do nothing to diminish the natural and
proper incentives to effort, and would not in any way
tend to diminish the sense of parental responsibility or
to weaken family ties.

The question arises, then—Is there any way in
which we may hope to see such an adjustment of
incomes brought about ? In a paper published many
years ago,[1] I suggested that the State and the municipalities, which employ a large and constantly increasing number of selected servants, should introduce remuneration on this plan into all their services. I urged
that, if this were done, public opinion would be quick
to recognize the essential justice, as well as the social
and eugenic expediency, of the plan, and would bring
such pressure to bear on all large employers of skilled
labour, that they might be led to follow suit. It is

[1] "A Practical Eugenic Suggestion," a paper read
before the British Sociological Society and published in
Sociological Papers, Vol. II, London, 1909.

interesting to note that, since my suggestion was made, some small steps have been taken in this direction ; though it is clear that these steps were due to recognition of their essential justice rather than to consideration of their eugenic effects ; for statesmen remain absolutely blind and ignorant in face of the eugenic problem. I refer more especially (1) to the small remissions of income tax made by the British Government on account of children of persons of small incomes ; (2) to the separation allowances paid to soldiers by the British and other governments during the war. In the British army these allowances were made larger in proportion to the number of children and in proportion to the rank and pay of the soldier ; so that a sergeant-major, for example, with a large family received a very much larger pay than an unmarried private. This was essentially just, and was generally approved ; and it was also eugenic. But that the eugenic consideration played no part in determining this scale seems clear from the fact that (until near the end of the war, when some slight change was made) the plan was not applied to the commissioned officers. The British Government thus let slip an opportunity to put in practice a eugenic measure of tremendous power, which would have been universally welcomed and approved, and which would have done something to compensate for the terrible losses of human qualities which the country suffered in the war. For there, in the commissioned ranks, were practically all the most capable and healthy young men of the British Empire, all the most desirable fathers, selected from all the manhood of the Empire by the stringent tests of achievement in the field and success in the officers' training-schools. The ignorance and folly of a government which let pass this opportunity, while recognizing in its treatment of the non-commissioned ranks the essential justice of this plan of remuneration, is

198

deplorable, both on account of the grave injustice done to so many brave men and on account of the many fine children they might have fathered under the plan, but who were never conceived.[1] Yet, in spite of the loss of this great opportunity and of the official ignoring of the eugenic effects of remuneration on the new plan, the fact that it was applied throughout the non-commissioned ranks is very encouraging; for it constituted official recognition of the justice of this plan and familiarized the public with the principle.

I can see no reason why, in this and in every civilized country, this new plan of remuneration should not be applied forthwith to every State and municipal service, with great eugenic effects. But I recognize difficulties in the way of supposing that the same plan might be universally or widely adopted by private firms or by public and semi-public corporations and institutions not supported by taxation. Let us consider the case of the teachers in those educational institutions which are not wholly supported by public funds. To make the problem more concrete, let us take the case of the teachers in endowed universities or colleges, institutions which, next to the State and the municipalities, might be expected to be most readily moved by enlightened regard for eugenic principles. The governing body has at its disposal a certain amount of income for payment of salaries. It rightly desires to include in the faculty the largest possible number of men of high ability and achievement. Two candidates for a post appear to be equally well qualified; but one of them is a bachelor, or has a small family; the other, though of the same age, already has a large family. Which will be appointed, if the " new plan " has been adopted ? Similar difficulties in the working

[1] There were non-commissioned officers with families who refused to accept commissions because they could not afford to do so.

of the plan would arise in—and would be even more serious in—any corporation whose primary aim was the making of profits. It is perhaps hardly to be hoped that—even if the " new plan " were enforced by legislation in the public services, the army, the navy, the civil service, the municipal services, and so forth— example and the force of public opinion could secure its effective adoption in the remuneration of all selected classes of workers. What possibilities of its general adoption remain ? I can think of two only, or rather two varieties of one scheme ; namely, the setting apart of a national fund for the supplementing of salaries of selected workers according to the " new plan." This national fund might be provided by taxation ; or it might be created, and increased from time to time, by the public spirit and beneficence of rich men. We have already seen the late Andrew Carnegie provide a pensions fund for selected university professors. May we not hope for the realization of this more far-reaching scheme, which, from the points of view of both social justice and national welfare, would be so admirable. I can think of no other purpose to which the rich man who wishes to promote the welfare of his kind, both in the present and for all time, could so confidently devote his wealth, without risk of pauperizing any individual or of doing any social injury that might offset the benefits he aimed to confer on his fellow men. In order to make the " new plan " as wide in its operation as is desirable, a very large sum would be required ; but in the first instance it might be applied to some one highly selected class, such as the teachers in colleges and universities. For not only are such teachers in the main a very highly selected class, embodying much of the best human qualities of the whole country ; they are also notoriously a class which is restricted in reproduction by the narrowness of its means ; and they are a class whose remuneration is in the hands of responsible governing bodies, which might be trusted to administer with discretion and fairness any moneys derived from " the national fund for the new plan."

In view of the difficulty of moving legislatures to action directed to the good of posterity, it seems probable that the best hope of instituting the new plan lies in the possibility of raising the required national fund by appeal to private beneficence. It might be hoped that, if in this way a beginning were once made, the State might later be led to appreciate the value of the new plan, to adopt it in the payment of all public servants, and to create the large national fund necessary for its general application on the widest possible scale.

If the new plan were adopted in Great Britain, it might save some remnants of the old professional class which, the product of a long process of selection, has been the repository of a very large proportion of the best qualities of the British stock and the source of most of the leaders in all departments of the national life. This class, on which the burdens of the war fell more heavily than on any other, is now being rapidly taxed out of existence.

APPENDIX IV

Registration of Family Histories

ALTHOUGH I regard the " new plan " sketched in Appendix III as the most important eugenic measure that can be advocated with any hope of success, I recognize that we cannot afford to neglect any other measure of eugenic tendency ; and I propose here another such reform which, as public opinion becomes enlightened, might be of great value, and might be put into operation without great cost and without any interference with the liberty of the individual. I suggest that the State should institute a voluntary registration of family histories, and should keep, in clear and easily consulted form, a record of all family histories thus registered.

It is one of the gravest evils of the present time, and a source of terrible hardship to many persons, that, in choosing a wife or a husband, the choice has so often to be made in almost complete ignorance of important facts in the family history of the individual concerned. Many a man (and woman) has found himself united to a partner whose family history betrays a strong tendency to insanity, tuberculosis, or alcohol, or some other grave defect.

If such voluntary registration were instituted, and if the State made every effort, by the aid of properly equipped officials, to verify and check the accuracy of the recorded information, it would, I think, soon become the custom, for all or most of the more educated part of the

14*

community, to register each child in its proper place in the genealogical tables, and to consult these tables (at a small fee, perhaps) when engagement or marriage was contemplated. Even if the young people concerned were slow, in many cases, to take advantage of the information thus rendered available, their parents might be trusted to pay more attention to it and, in the light of it, to give wise advice, which, when so well founded, would not fail to carry weight. When the system had been in operation for some little time, the mere absence of any family record in the official tables would afford a strong presumption of the existence of some grave defect in the family concerned and would be a ground for caution and further inquiry. That very many persons are not averse from such recording of their family histories, and even their publication at large, is shown by the columns devoted to genealogies of citizens in some of the leading newspapers of America.

Some of the most prominent advocates of eugenic measures have been bachelors or childless men, and in some cases they have been persons whose family relations have in other ways departed from the normal and generally desirable type. It thus happens that the eugenists have been laid open to the retort—Why don't you practise what you preach? In order to defend myself in advance from any such reproach, I publish a little picture of my children as they appeared in the year 1914.

APPENDIX VI

I ADD a short list of the books which seem to me best suited to give the general reader further information concerning the main topic discussed in the foregoing pages :

"Applied Eugenics," by Paul Popenoe (editor of the *Journal of Heredity*) and R. H. Johnson. New York : The Macmillan Co., 1918.

This is, I think, the best general discussion of eugenic problems and principles for the general reader.

"The Racial Prospect," by S. K. Humphrey. New York : Charles Scribner's Sons, 1920 ; and "Mankind," by the same author and publisher, 1917.

These two books are excellent discussions of human qualities, with special reference to the future in America.

"The Old World in the New," by E. A. Ross (Professor of Sociology in the University of Wisconsin). New York : The Century Co., 1914.

A discussion of "The Significance of Past and Present Immigration to the American People." The author cites many facts of observation and many weighty opinions which illustrate the reality of racial peculiarities and their persistence and influence under changed environment. The careful reader will see that these, in the main, agree closely with the evidence and findings of my pages ; compare, e.g., what is said on pages

113 *et seq.* on the low level of intelligence and the character traits of the immigrants from Southern Italy. It is much to be desired that every American citizen should read this book with an open mind. Says this high authority : " Not until the twenty-first century will the philosophic historian be able to declare with scientific certitude that the cause of the mysterious decline that came upon the American people early in the twentieth century was the deterioration of popular intelligence by the admission of great numbers of backward immigrants."

" The Direction of Human Evolution," by E. G. Conklin (Professor of Biology in Princeton University). New York : Charles Scribner's Sons, 1921.

An excellent popular discussion of human and racial qualities from the eugenic and political point of view by a distinguished biologist.

" Population and Birth Control," edited by E. and C. Paul. New York : The Critic and Guide Company, 1917.

Written by a dozen writers of widely dissimilar views, this book contains a very thorough and well-balanced discussion of that all-important topic, birth control, its eugenic and dysgenic tendencies and possibilities.

" The Revolutions of Civilization," by Professor Flinders Petrie. New York : Harper Bros., 1919.

An impressive picture of the rise and fall of civilizations by this eminent archæologist and Egyptologist.

This is only a small selection from a large and rapidly increasing literature. I wish to point out to readers that they are not to regard this selection as one-sided and biased. The most striking fact about the present situation is that, while popular and journalistic opinion refuses in the main to face the racial problem and to take seriously the propaganda of the eugenists, all the facts, all authority, and all instructed and weighty opinion converge to show the supreme importance of this problem and of this propaganda.

INDEX

211

INDEX

National character, 53
National fund, 200
National institutions, 151
Negro, the, intelligence of, 71, 74 ; moral qualities of, 127
Neo-Darwinism, 135
Nervous troubles, 99
New factor, 174
New knowledge, effects of, 28
New plan, 191–201
Newsholme, 188
Nordic race, the, 50 ; curiosity of, 96 ; self-assertion of, 124
Normans, 123

Oakesmith, J., 52, 55
Old age of nations, 41
Oxford experiment, 77

Parabola of peoples, 31, 160
Pater, Walter, 92
Paul, E. and C., 208
Pearson, K., 77, 167, 188
Persistence of qualities, 146
Personal relations, 37
Petrie, Flinders, 30, 34, 208
Physical energies, control of, 35, 36
Pittsburgh, 188
Plato, 191
Popenoe, P., 167, 188, 191, 207
Portuguese, the, 80
Pressey, S. L., 74, 81
Professional classes, 200, 201
Protestants, 112, 125
Providence, 129
Psychoanalysts, 136

Quessel, L., 163

Race, H. V., 142
Race blending, 34
Race-dogmatists, 47
Race hatred, 49
Race and intelligence, 73

Race problem, 42
Race-slumpers, 51, 55
Race suicide, 163, 195
Races, European, 87
Ralston, R., 81
Red men, 126
Registration of family histories, 203
Reid, Archdall, 100
Religion and race, 112
Responsibility, 175
Reversion, 152
Ripley, Z., 57, 103, 105, 146
Robertson, J. M., 55
Roman Empire, 33
Romans, 93
Romantic art, 92
Rome, 172
Ross, E. A., 207

Seeck, Otto, 93, 172
Selection, 154
Shaler, N. S., 72, 73, 75, 128, 138
Sheffield, 185
Slavery, 37
Sociability, 94
Social ladder, 155, 158, 162
Social status and intelligence, 79, 156
Social strata in America, 78
Spain, 173
Spaniards, the, 80
Spencer, H., 159
Standard demands, 195
State register, 203
Statistical statements, 55
Stature, distribution of, 57
Stevenson, 188
Suicide, 105

Terman, S. M., 80, 81, 141, 165
Tests, mental, 63
Teter, G. F., 74
Times, the London, 120, 161

213

Printed in Great Britain by Butler & Tanner, *Frome and London*

A SELECTION FROM
MESSRS. METHUEN'S
PUBLICATIONS

This Catalogue contains only a selection of the more important books published by Messrs. Methuen. A complete catalogue of their publications may be obtained on application.

Bain (F. W.)—
A DIGIT OF THE MOON: A Hindoo Love Story. THE DESCENT OF THE SUN: A Cycle of Birth. A HEIFER OF THE DAWN. IN THE GREAT GOD'S HAIR. A DRAUGHT OF THE BLUE. AN ESSENCE OF THE DUSK. AN INCARNATION OF THE SNOW. A MINE OF FAULTS. THE ASHES OF A GOD. BUBBLES OF THE FOAM. A SYRUP OF THE BEES. THE LIVERY OF EVE. THE SUBSTANCE OF A DREAM. *All Fcap. 8vo. 5s. net.* AN ECHO OF THE SPHERES. *Wide Demy. 12s. 6d. net.*

Baker (C. H. Collins). CROME. Illustrated. *Quarto. £5. 5s. net.*

Balfour (Sir Graham). THE LIFE OF ROBERT LOUIS STEVENSON. *Fifteenth Edition. In one Volume. Cr. 8vo. Buckram, 7s. 6d. net.*

Belloc (H.)—
PARIS, 8s. 6d. net. HILLS AND THE SEA, 6s. net. ON NOTHING AND KINDRED SUBJECTS, 6s. net. ON EVERYTHING, 6s. net. ON SOMETHING, 6s. net. FIRST AND LAST, 6s. net. THIS AND THAT AND THE OTHER, 6s. net. MARIE ANTOINETTE, 18s. net. THE PYRENEES, 10s. 6d. net.

Blackmore (S. Powell). LAWN TENNIS UP-TO-DATE. Illustrated. *Demy 8vo. 12s. 6d. net.*

Campbell (Norman R.). WHAT IS SCIENCE? *Cr. 8vo. 5s. net.*

Chandler (Arthur), D.D., late Lord Bishop of Bloemfontein—
ARA CŒLI: An Essay in Mystical Theology, 5s. net. FAITH AND EXPERIENCE, 5s. net. THE CULT OF THE PASSING MOMENT, 5s. net. THE ENGLISH CHURCH AND REUNION, 5s. net. SCALA MUNDI, 4s. 6d. net.

Chesterton (G. K.)—
THE BALLAD OF THE WHITE HORSE. ALL THINGS CONSIDERED. TREMENDOUS TRIFLES. ALARMS AND DISCURSIONS. A MISCELLANY OF MEN. THE USES OF DIVERSITY. *All Fcap. 8vo. 6s. net.* WINE, WATER, AND SONG. *Fcap. 8vo. 1s. 6d. net.*

Clutton-Brock (A.). WHAT IS THE KINGDOM OF HEAVEN? *Fifth Edition. Fcap. 8vo 5s. net.*
ESSAYS ON ART. *Second Edition. Fcap. 8vo. 5s. net.*
ESSAYS ON BOOKS. *Third Edition. Fcap. 8vo. 6s. net.*
MORE ESSAYS ON BOOKS. *Fcap. 8vo. 6s. net.*

Cole (G. D. H.). SOCIAL THEORY. *Second Edition, revised. Cr. 8vo. 6s. net.*

Conrad (Joseph). THE MIRROR OF THE SEA: Memories and Impressions *Fourth Edition. Fcap. 8vo. 6s. net.*

Drever (James). THE PSYCHOLOGY OF EVERYDAY LIFE. *Cr. 8vo. 6s. net.*
THE PSYCHOLOGY OF INDUSTRY. *Cr. 8vo. 5s. net.*

Einstein (A.). RELATIVITY: THE SPECIAL AND THE GENERAL THEORY. Translated by ROBERT W. LAWSON. *Sixth Edition. Cr. 8vo. 5s. net.*

Other Books on the **Einstein Theory.**

SPACE—TIME—MATTER. By HERMANN WEYL. *Demy 8vo. 21s. net.*
EINSTEIN THE SEARCHER: HIS WORK EXPLAINED IN DIALOGUES WITH EINSTEIN. By ALEXANDER MOSZKOWSKI. *Demy 8vo. 12s. 6d. net.*
AN INTRODUCTION TO THE THEORY OF RELATIVITY. By LYNDON BOLTON. *Cr. 8vo. 5s. net.*
RELATIVITY AND GRAVITATION. By various Writers. Edited by J. MALCOLM BIRD. *Cr. 8vo. 7s. 6d. net.*
RELATIVITY AND THE UNIVERSE. By Dr. HARRY SCHMIDT. *Cr. 8vo. 5s. net.*

Fyleman (Rose). FAIRIES AND CHIMNEYS. *Fcap. 8vo. Ninth Edition. 3s. 6d. net.*
THE FAIRY GREEN. *Fourth Edition. Fcap. 8vo. 3s. 6d. net.*
THE FAIRY FLUTE. *Fcap. 8vo. 3s. 6d. net.*

Gibbins (H. de B.). INDUSTRY IN ENGLAND: HISTORICAL OUTLINES. With Maps and Plans. *Tenth Edition. Demy 8vo. 12s. 6d. net.*
THE INDUSTRIAL HISTORY OF ENGLAND. With 5 Maps and a Plan. *Twenty-seventh Edition. Cr. 8vo. 5s.*

Gibbon (Edward). THE DECLINE AND FALL OF THE ROMAN EMPIRE. Edited, with Notes, Appendices, and Maps, by J. B. BURY. *Seven Volumes. Demy 8vo. Illustrated. Each 12s. 6d. net. Also in Seven Volumes. Unillustrated. Cr. 8vo. Each 7s. 6d. net.*

Glover (T. R.)—
THE CONFLICT OF RELIGIONS IN THE EARLY ROMAN EMPIRE, 10s. 6d. net. POETS AND PURITANS, 10s. 6d. net. FROM PERICLES TO PHILIP, 10s. 6d. net. VIRGIL, 10s. 6d. net. THE CHRISTIAN TRADITION AND ITS VERIFICATION (The Angus Lecture for 1912), 6s. net.

Grahame (Kenneth). THE WIND IN THE WILLOWS. *Eleventh Edition. Cr. 8vo. 7s. 6d. net.*

Hall (H. R.). THE ANCIENT HISTORY OF THE NEAR EAST FROM THE EARLIEST TIMES TO THE BATTLE OF SALAMIS. Illustrated. *Fifth Edition. Demy 8vo. 21s. net.*

Hawthorne (Nathaniel). THE SCARLET LETTER. With 31 Illustrations in Colour by HUGH THOMSON. *Wide Royal 8vo. 31s. 6d. net.*

Herbert (A. P.). THE WHEREFORE AND THE WHY: NEW RHYMES FOR OLD CHILDREN. Illustrated by GEORGE MORROW. *Fcap. 4to. 3s. 6d. net.*

LIGHT ARTICLES ONLY. Illustrated by GEORGE MORROW. *Cr. 8vo. 6s. net.*

Holdsworth (W. S.). A HISTORY OF ENGLISH LAW. *Vols. I., II., III. Each Second Edition. Demy 8vo. Each 15s. net.*

Inge (W. R.). CHRISTIAN MYSTICISM. (The Bampton Lectures of 1899.) *Fifth Edition. Cr. 8vo. 7s. 6d. net.*

Jenks (E.). AN OUTLINE OF ENGLISH LOCAL GOVERNMENT. *Fourth Edition.* Revised by R. C. K. ENSOR. *Cr. 8vo. 5s. net.*

A SHORT HISTORY OF ENGLISH LAW: FROM THE EARLIEST TIMES TO THE END OF THE YEAR 1911. *Second Edition, revised. Demy 8vo. 12s. 6d. net.*

Julian (Lady) of Norwich. REVELATIONS OF DIVINE LOVE. Edited by GRACE WARRACK. *Seventh Edition. Cr. 8vo. 5s. net.*

Keats (John). POEMS. Edited, with Introduction and Notes, by E. DE SÉLINCOURT. With a Frontispiece in Photogravure. *Fourth Edition. Demy 8vo. 12s. 6d. net.*

Kidd (Benjamin). THE SCIENCE OF POWER. *Ninth Edition. Crown 8vo. 6s. net.*

SOCIAL EVOLUTION. *Demy 8vo. 8s. 6d. net.*

A PHILOSOPHER WITH NATURE. *Cr. 8vo. 7s. 6d. net.*

Kipling (Rudyard). BARRACK-ROOM BALLADS. 215th Thousand. *Cr. 8vo. Buckram, 7s. 6d. net. Also Fcap. 8vo. Cloth, 6s. net; leather, 7s. 6d. net.* Also a Service Edition. *Two Volumes. Square fcap. 8vo. Each 3s. net.*

THE SEVEN SEAS. 157th Thousand. *Cr. 8vo. Buckram, 7s. 6d. net. Also Fcap. 8vo. Cloth, 6s. net; leather, 7s. 6d. net.* Also a Service Edition. *Two Volumes. Square fcap. 8vo. Each 3s. net.*

Kipling (Rudyard)—*continued.*
THE FIVE NATIONS. 126th Thousand. *Cr. 8vo. Buckram, 7s. 6d. net. Also Fcap. 8vo. Cloth, 6s. net; leather, 7s. 6d. net.* Also a Service Edition. *Two Volumes. Square fcap. 8vo. Each 3s. net.*

DEPARTMENTAL DITTIES. 102nd Thousand. *Cr. 8vo. Buckram, 7s. 6d. net. Also Fcap. 8vo. Cloth, 6s. net; leather, 7s. 6d. net.* Also a Service Edition. *Two Volumes. Square fcap. 8vo. Each 3s. net.*

THE YEARS BETWEEN. 95th Thousand. *Cr. 8vo. Buckram, 7s. 6d. net. Fcap. 8vo. Blue cloth, 6s. net; Limp lambskin, 7s. 6d. net.* Also a Service Edition. *Two Volumes. Square fcap. 8vo. Each 3s. net.*

HYMN BEFORE ACTION. Illuminated. *Fcap. 4to. 1s. 6d. net.*

RECESSIONAL. Illuminated. *Fcap. 4to 1s. 6d. net.*

TWENTY POEMS FROM RUDYARD KIPLING. 360th Thousand. *Fcap. 8vo. 1s. net.*

SELECTED POEMS. *Cr. 8vo. 5s. net.*

Knox (E. V. G.). ('Evoe' of *Punch*.) PARODIES REGAINED. Illustrated by GEORGE MORROW. *Fcap. 8vo. 6s. net.*

Lamb (Charles and Mary). THE COMPLETE WORKS. Edited by E. V. LUCAS. *A New and Revised Edition in Six Volumes. With Frontispieces. Fcap. 8vo. Each 6s. net.*
The volumes are :—
I. MISCELLANEOUS PROSE. II. ELIA AND THE LAST ESSAY OF ELIA. III. BOOKS FOR CHILDREN. IV. PLAYS AND POEMS. V. and VI. LETTERS.

THE ESSAYS OF ELIA. With an Introduction by E. V. LUCAS, and 28 Illustration by A. GARTH JONES. *Fcap. 8vo. 5s. net.*

Lankester (Sir Ray). SCIENCE FROM AN EASY CHAIR. Illustrated. *Thirteenth Edition. Cr. 8vo. 7s. 6d. net.*

SCIENCE FROM AN EASY CHAIR. *Second Series.* Illustrated. *Third Edition. Cr. 8vo. 7s. 6d. net.*

DIVERSIONS OF A NATURALIST. Illustrated. *Third Edition. Cr. 8vo. 7s. 6d. net.*

SECRETS OF EARTH AND SEA. *Cr. 8vo. 8s. 6d. net.*

Lodge (Sir Oliver). MAN AND THE UNIVERSE: A STUDY OF THE INFLUENCE OF THE ADVANCE IN SCIENTIFIC KNOWLEDGE UPON OUR UNDERSTANDING OF CHRISTIANITY. *Ninth Edition. Crown 8vo. 7s. 6d. net.*

THE SURVIVAL OF MAN: A STUDY IN UNRECOGNISED HUMAN FACULTY. *Seventh Edition. Cr. 8vo. 7s. 6d. net.*

MODERN PROBLEMS. *Cr. 8vo. 7s. 6d. net.*

RAYMOND; OR LIFE AND DEATH. Illustrated. *Twelfth Edition. Demy 8vo. 15s. net.*

Lucas (E. V.)—
THE LIFE OF CHARLES LAMB, 2 *vols.*, 21*s. net.* A WANDERER IN HOLLAND, 10*s. 6d. net.* A WANDERER IN LONDON, 10*s. 6d. net.* LONDON REVISITED, 10*s. 6d. net.* A WANDERER IN PARIS, 10*s. 6d. net* and 6*s. net.* A WANDERER IN FLORENCE, 10*s. 6d. net.* A WANDERER IN VENICE, 10*s. 6d. net.* THE OPEN ROAD: A Little Book for Wayfarers, 6*s. 6d. net* and 21*s. net.* THE FRIENDLY TOWN: A Little Book for the Urbane, 6*s. net.* FIRESIDE AND SUNSHINE, 6*s. net.* CHARACTER AND COMEDY, 6*s. net.* THE GENTLEST ART: A Choice of Letters by Entertaining Hands, 6*s. 6d. net.* THE SECOND POST, 6*s. net.* HER INFINITE VARIETY: A Feminine Portrait Gallery, 6*s. net.* GOOD COMPANY: A Rally of Men, 6*s. net.* ONE DAY AND ANOTHER, 6*s. net.* OLD LAMPS FOR NEW, 6*s. net.* LOITERER'S HARVEST, 6*s. net.* CLOUD AND SILVER, 6*s. net.* A BOSWELL OF BAGHDAD, AND OTHER ESSAYS, 6*s. net.* 'TWIXT EAGLE AND DOVE, 6*s. net.* THE PHANTOM JOURNAL, AND OTHER ESSAYS AND DIVERSIONS, 6*s. net.* SPECIALLY SELECTED: A Choice of Essays. 7*s. 6d. net.* THE BRITISH SCHOOL: An Anecdotal Guide to the British Painters and Paintings in the National Gallery, 6*s. net.* ROVING EAST AND ROVING WEST: Notes gathered in India, Japan, and America. 5*s. net.* URBANITIES. Illustrated by G. L. Stampa, 7*s. 6d. net.* VERMEER, 10*s. 6d. net.*

M.(A.). AN ANTHOLOGY OF MODERN VERSE. With Introduction by ROBERT LYND. *Third Edition. Fcap. 8vo.* 6*s. net. Thin paper, leather,* 7*s. 6d. net.*

McDougall (William). AN INTRODUCTION TO SOCIAL PSYCHOLOGY. *Sixteenth Edition. Cr. 8vo.* 8*s. 6d. net.*
BODY AND MIND: A HISTORY AND A DEFENCE OF ANIMISM. *Fifth Edition. Demy 8vo.* 12*s. 6d. net.*

MacIver (R. M.). THE ELEMENTS OF SOCIAL SCIENCE. *Cr. 8vo.* 6*s. net.*

Maeterlinck (Maurice)—
THE BLUE BIRD: A Fairy Play in Six Acts, 6*s. net.* MARY MAGDALENE: A Play in Three Acts, 5*s. net.* DEATH, 3*s. 6d. net.* OUR ETERNITY, 6*s. net.* THE UNKNOWN GUEST, 6*s. net.* POEMS, 5*s. net.* THE WRACK OF THE STORM, 6*s. net.* THE MIRACLE OF ST. ANTHONY: A Play in One Act, 3*s. 6d. net.* THE BURGOMASTER OF STILEMONDE: A Play in Three Acts, 5*s. net.* THE BETROTHAL; or, The Blue Bird Chooses, 6*s. net.* MOUNTAIN PATHS, 6*s. net.* THE STORY OF TYLTYL, 21*s. net.*

Milne (A. A.). THE DAY'S PLAY. THE HOLIDAY ROUND. ONCE A WEEK. *All Cr. 8vo.* 7*s. 6d. net.* NOT THAT IT MATTERS. *Fcap. 8vo.* 6*s. net.* IF I MAY. *Fcap. 8vo.* 6*s. net.* THE SUNNY SIDE. *Fcap. 8vo.* 6*s. net.*

Oxenham (John)—
BEES IN AMBER; A Little Book of Thoughtful Verse. ALL'S WELL: A Collection of War Poems. THE KING'S HIGH WAY. THE VISION SPLENDID. THE FIERY CROSS. HIGH ALTARS: The Record of a Visit to the Battlefields of France and Flanders. HEARTS COURAGEOUS. ALL CLEAR! *All Small Pott 8vo. Paper,* 1*s. 3d. net; cloth boards,* 2*s. net.* WINDS OF THE DAWN. GENTLEMEN—THE KING, 2*s. net.*

Petrie (W. M. Flinders). A HISTORY OF EGYPT. Illustrated. *Six Volumes. Cr. 8vo. Each* 9*s. net.*
VOL. I. FROM THE 1ST TO THE XVITH DYNASTY. *Ninth Edition.* (10*s. 6d. net.*)
VOL. II. THE XVIITH AND XVIIITH DYNASTIES. *Sixth Edition.*
VOL. III. XIXTH TO XXXTH DYNASTIES. *Second Edition.*
VOL. IV. EGYPT UNDER THE PTOLEMAIC DYNASTY. J. P. MAHAFFY. *Second Edition.*
VOL. V. EGYPT UNDER ROMAN RULE. J. G. MILNE. *Second Edition.*
VOL. VI. EGYPT IN THE MIDDLE AGES. STANLEY LANE POOLE. *Second Edition.*
SYRIA AND EGYPT, FROM THE TELL EL AMARNA LETTERS. *Cr. 8vo.* 5*s. net.*
EGYPTIAN TALES. Translated from the Papyri. First Series, IVTH to XIITH Dynasty. Illustrated. *Third Edition. Cr. 8vo.* 5*s. net.*
EGYPTIAN TALES. Translated from the Papyri. Second Series, XVIIITH to XIXTH Dynasty. Illustrated. *Second Edition. Cr. 8vo.* 5*s. net.*

Pollard (A. F.). A SHORT HISTORY OF THE GREAT WAR. With 19 Maps. *Second Edition. Cr. 8vo.* 10*s. 6d. net.*

Pollitt (Arthur W.). THE ENJOYMENT OF MUSIC. *Cr. 8vo.* 5*s. net.*

Price (L. L.). A SHORT HISTORY OF POLITICAL ECONOMY IN ENGLAND FROM ADAM SMITH TO ARNOLD TOYNBEE. *Tenth Edition. Cr. 8vo.* 5*s. net.*

Reid (G. Archdall). THE LAWS OF HEREDITY. *Second Edition. Demy 8vo.* £1 1*s. net.*

Robertson (C. Grant). SELECT STATUTES, CASES, AND DOCUMENTS, 1660–1832. *Third Edition. Demy 8vo.* 15*s. net.*

Selous (Edmund)—
TOMMY SMITH'S ANIMALS, 3*s. 6d. net.* TOMMY SMITH'S OTHER ANIMALS, 3*s. 6d. net.* TOMMY SMITH AT THE ZOO, 2*s. 9d.* TOMMY SMITH AGAIN AT THE ZOO, 2*s. 9d.* JACK'S INSECTS, 3*s. 6d.* JACK'S OTHER INSECTS, 3*s. 6d.*

Shelley (Percy Bysshe). POEMS. With an Introduction by A. CLUTTON-BROCK and Notes by C. D. LOCOCK. *Two Volumes. Demy 8vo.* £1 1*s. net.*

Smith (Adam). THE WEALTH OF NATIONS. Edited by EDWIN CANNAN. *Two Volumes. Second Edition. Demy 8vo. £1 10s. net.*

Smith (S. C. Kaines). LOOKING AT PICTURES. Illustrated. *Fcap. 8vo. 6s. net.*

Stevenson (R. L.). THE LETTERS OF ROBERT LOUIS STEVENSON. Edited by Sir SIDNEY COLVIN. *A New Rearranged Edition in four volumes. Fourth Edition. Fcap. 8vo. Each 6s. net.*

Surtees (R. S.)—
HANDLEY CROSS, 7s. 6d. net. MR. SPONGE'S SPORTING TOUR, 7s. 6d. net. ASK MAMMA: or, The Richest Commoner in England, 7s. 6d. net. JORROCKS'S JAUNTS AND JOLLITIES, 6s. net. MR. FACEY ROMFORD'S HOUNDS, 7s. 6d. net. HAWBUCK GRANGE; or, The Sporting Adventures of Thomas Scott, Esq., 6s. net. PLAIN OR RINGLETS? 7s. 6d. net. HILLINGDON HALL, 7s. 6d. net.

Tilden (W. T.). THE ART OF LAWN TENNIS. Illustrated. *Third Edition. Cr. 8vo. 6s. net.*

Tileston (Mary W.). DAILY STRENGTH FOR DAILY NEEDS. *Twenty-seventh Edition. Medium 16mo. 3s. 6d. net.*

Townshend (R. B.). INSPIRED GOLF. *Fcap. 8vo. 2s. 6d. net.*

Turner (W. J.). MUSIC AND LIFE. *Crown 8vo. 7s. 6d. net.*

Underhill (Evelyn). MYSTICISM. A Study in the Nature and Development of Man's Spiritual Consciousness. *Eighth Edition. Demy 8vo. 15s. net.*

Vardon (Harry). HOW TO PLAY GOLF. Illustrated. *Fourteenth Edition. Cr. 8vo. 5s. 6d. net.*

Waterhouse (Elizabeth). A LITTLE BOOK OF LIFE AND DEATH. *Twenty-first Edition. Small Pott 8vo. Cloth, 2s. 6d. net.*

Wells (J.). A SHORT HISTORY OF ROME. *Seventeenth Edition.* With 3 Maps. *Cr. 8vo. 6s.*

Wilde (Oscar). THE WORKS OF OSCAR WILDE. *Fcap. 8vo. Each 6s. 6d. net.*
I. LORD ARTHUR SAVILE'S CRIME AND THE PORTRAIT OF MR. W. H. II. THE DUCHESS OF PADUA. III. POEMS. IV. LADY WINDERMERE'S FAN. V. A WOMAN OF NO IMPORTANCE. VI. AN IDEAL HUSBAND. VII. THE IMPORTANCE OF BEING EARNEST. VIII. A HOUSE OF POMEGRANATES. IX. INTENTIONS. X. DE PROFUNDIS AND PRISON LETTERS. XI. ESSAYS. XII. SALOMÉ, A FLORENTINE TRAGEDY, and LA SAINTE COURTISANE. XIII. A CRITIC IN PALL MALL. XIV. SELECTED PROSE OF OSCAR WILDE. XV. ART AND DECORATION.

A HOUSE OF POMEGRANATES. Illustrated. *Cr. 4to. 21s. net.*

Yeats (W. B.). A BOOK OF IRISH VERSE. *Fourth Edition. Cr. 8vo. 7s. net.*

PART II.—A SELECTION OF SERIES

Ancient Cities

General Editor, SIR B. C. A. WINDLE

Cr. 8vo. 6s. net each volume

With Illustrations by E. H. NEW, and other Artists

BRISTOL. CANTERBURY. CHESTER. DUBLIN. | EDINBURGH. LINCOLN. SHREWSBURY.

The Antiquary's Books

Demy 8vo. 10s. 6d. net each volume

With Numerous Illustrations

ANCIENT PAINTED GLASS IN ENGLAND. ARCHÆOLOGY AND FALSE ANTIQUITIES. THE BELLS OF ENGLAND. THE BRASSES OF ENGLAND. THE CASTLES AND WALLED TOWNS OF ENGLAND. CELTIC ART IN PAGAN AND CHRISTIAN TIMES. CHURCHWARDENS' ACCOUNTS. THE DOMESDAY INQUEST. ENGLISH CHURCH FURNITURE. ENGLISH COSTUME. ENGLISH MONASTIC LIFE. ENGLISH SEALS. FOLK-LORE AS AN HISTORICAL SCIENCE. THE GILDS AND COMPANIES OF LONDON. THE HERMITS AND ANCHORITES OF ENGLAND. THE MANOR AND MANORIAL RECORDS. THE MEDIÆVAL HOSPITALS OF ENGLAND. OLD ENGLISH INSTRUMENTS OF MUSIC. OLD ENGLISH LIBRARIES. OLD SERVICE BOOKS OF THE ENGLISH CHURCH. PARISH LIFE IN MEDIÆVAL ENGLAND. THE PARISH REGISTERS OF ENGLAND. REMAINS OF THE PREHISTORIC AGE IN ENGLAND. THE ROMAN ERA IN BRITAIN. ROMANO-BRITISH BUILDINGS AND EARTHWORKS. THE ROYAL FORESTS OF ENGLAND. THE SCHOOLS OF MEDIEVAL ENGLAND. SHRINES OF BRITISH SAINTS.

The Arden Shakespeare

General Editor, R. H. CASE

Demy 8vo. 6s. net each volume

An edition of Shakespeare in Single Plays ; each edited with a full Introduction, Textual Notes, and a Commentary at the foot of the page.

Classics of Art

Edited by Dr. J. H. W. LAING

With numerous Illustrations. Wide Royal 8vo

THE ART OF THE GREEKS, 15s. net. THE ART OF THE ROMANS, 16s. net. CHARDIN, 15s. net. DONATELLO, 16s. net. GEORGE ROMNEY, 15s. net. GHIRLANDAIO, 15s. net. LAWRENCE, 25s. net. MICHELANGELO, 15s. net. RAPHAEL, 15s. net. REMBRANDT'S ETCHINGS, 31s. 6d. net. REMBRANDT'S PAINTINGS, 42s. net. TINTORETTO, 16s. net. TITIAN, 16s. net. TURNER'S SKETCHES AND DRAWINGS, 15s. net. VELAZQUEZ, 15s. net.

The 'Complete' Series

Fully Illustrated. Demy 8vo

THE COMPLETE AIRMAN, 16s. net. THE COMPLETE AMATEUR BOXER, 10s. 6d. net. THE COMPLETE ASSOCIATION FOOTBALLER, 10s. 6d. net. THE COMPLETE ATHLETIC TRAINER, 10s. 6d. net. THE COMPLETE BILLIARD PLAYER, 12s. 6d. net. THE COMPLETE COOK, 10s. 6d. net. THE COMPLETE CRICKETER, 10s. 6d. net. THE COMPLETE FOXHUNTER, 16s. net. THE COMPLETE GOLFER, 12s. 6d. net. THE COMPLETE HOCKEY-PLAYER, 10s. 6d. net. THE COMPLETE HORSEMAN, 12s. 6d. net. THE COMPLETE JUJITSUAN. Cr. 8vo. 5s. net. THE COMPLETE LAWN TENNIS PLAYER, 12s. 6d. net. THE COMPLETE MOTORIST, 10s. 6d. net. THE COMPLETE MOUNTAINEER, 16s. net. THE COMPLETE OARSMAN, 15s. net. THE COMPLETE PHOTOGRAPHER, 15s. net. THE COMPLETE RUGBY FOOTBALLER, ON THE NEW ZEALAND SYSTEM, 12s. 6d. net. THE COMPLETE SHOT, 16s. net. THE COMPLETE SWIMMER, 10s. 6d. net. THE COMPLETE YACHTSMAN, 18s. net.

The Connoisseur's Library

With numerous Illustrations. Wide Royal 8vo. 31s. 6d. net each volume

ENGLISH COLOURED BOOKS. ETCHINGS. EUROPEAN ENAMELS. FINE BOOKS. GLASS. GOLDSMITHS' AND SILVERSMITHS' WORK. ILLUMINATED MANUSCRIPTS. IVORIES. JEWELLERY. MEZZOTINTS. MINIATURES. PORCELAIN. SEALS. WOOD SCULPTURE.

Handbooks of Theology

Demy 8vo

THE DOCTRINE OF THE INCARNATION, 15s. net. A HISTORY OF EARLY CHRISTIAN DOCTRINE, 16s. net. INTRODUCTION TO THE HISTORY OF RELIGION, 12s. 6d. net. AN INTRODUCTION TO THE HISTORY OF THE CREEDS, 12s. 6d. net. THE PHILOSOPHY OF RELIGION IN ENGLAND AND AMERICA, 12s. 6d. net. THE XXXIX ARTICLES OF THE CHURCH OF ENGLAND, 15s. net.

Health Series

Fcap. 8vo. 2s. 6d. net

THE BABY. THE CARE OF THE BODY. THE CARE OF THE TEETH. THE EYES OF OUR CHILDREN. HEALTH FOR THE MIDDLE-AGED. THE HEALTH OF A WOMAN. THE HEALTH OF THE SKIN. HOW TO LIVE LONG. THE PREVENTION OF THE COMMON COLD. STAYING THE PLAGUE. THROAT AND EAR TROUBLES. TUBERCULOSIS. THE HEALTH OF THE CHILD. 2s. net.

The Library of Devotion

Handy Editions of the great Devotional Books, well edited.
With Introductions and (where necessary) Notes

Small Pott 8vo, cloth, 3s. net and 3s. 6d. net

Little Books on Art

With many Illustrations. Demy 16mo. 5s. net each volume

Each volume consists of about 200 pages, and contains from 30 to 40 Illustrations, including a Frontispiece in Photogravure

ALBRECHT DÜRER. THE ARTS OF JAPAN. BOOKPLATES. BOTTICELLI. BURNE-JONES. CELLINI. CHRISTIAN SYMBOLISM. CHRIST IN ART. CLAUDE. CONSTABLE. COROT. EARLY ENGLISH WATER-COLOUR. ENAMELS. FREDERIC LEIGHTON. GEORGE ROMNEY. GREEK ART. GREUZE AND

BOUCHER. HOLBEIN. ILLUMINATED MANUSCRIPTS. JEWELLERY. JOHN HOPPNER. Sir JOSHUA REYNOLDS. MILLET. MINIATURES. OUR LADY IN ART. RAPHAEL. RODIN. TURNER. VANDYCK. VELAZQUEZ. WATTS.

The Little Guides

With many Illustrations by E. H. NEW and other artists, and from photographs

Small Pott 8vo. 4s. net, 5s. net, and 6s. net

Guides to the English and Welsh Counties, and some well-known districts

The main features of these Guides are (1) a handy and charming form ; (2) illustrations from photographs and by well-known artists ; (3) good plans and maps ; (4) an adequate but compact presentation of everything that is interesting in the natural features, history, archæology, and architecture of the town or district treated.

The Little Quarto Shakespeare

Edited by W. J. CRAIG. With Introductions and Notes

Pott 16mo. 40 Volumes. Leather, price 1s. 9d. net each volume
Cloth, 1s. 6d.

Plays

Fcap. 8vo. 3s. 6d. net

MILESTONES. Arnold Bennett and Edward Knoblock. *Ninth Edition.*
IDEAL HUSBAND, AN. Oscar Wilde. *Acting Edition.*
KISMET. Edward Knoblock. *Fourth Edition.*
THE GREAT ADVENTURE. Arnold Bennett. *Fifth Edition.*

TYPHOON. A Play in Four Acts. Melchior Lengyel. English Version by Laurence Irving. *Second Edition.*
WARE CASE, THE. George Pleydell.
GENERAL POST. J. E. Harold Terry. *Second Edition.*
THE HONEYMOON. Arnold Bennett. *Third Edition.*

Sports Series

Illustrated. Fcap. 8vo

LL ABOUT FLYING, 3s. *net.* GOLF DO'S AND DONT'S, 2s. 6d. *net.* THE GOLFING SWING, 2s. 6d. *net.* QUICK CUTS TO GOOD GOLF, 2s. 6d. *net.* INSPIRED GOLF, 2s. 6d. *net.* HOW TO SWIM, 2s. *net.* LAWN TENNIS, 3s. *net.* SKATING, 3s. *net.* CROSS-COUNTRY SKI-ING, 5s. *net.* WRESTLING, 2s. *net.* HOCKEY, 4s. *net.*

The Westminster Commentaries

General Editor, WALTER LOCK

Demy 8vo

HE ACTS OF THE APOSTLES, 16s. *net.* AMOS, 8s. 6d. *net.* I. CORINTHIANS, 8s. 6d. *net.* EXODUS, 15s. *net.* EZEKIEL, 12s. 6d. *net.* GENESIS, 16s. *net.* HEBREWS, 8s. 6d. *net.* ISAIAH, 16s. *net.* JEREMIAH, 16s. *net.* JOB, 8s. 6d. *net.* THE PASTORAL EPISTLES, 8s. 6d. *net.* THE PHILIPPIANS, 8s. 6d. *net.* ST. JAMES, 8s. 6d. *net.* ST. MATTHEW, 15s. *net.*

Methuen's Two-Shilling Library

Cheap Editions of many Popular Books

Fcap. 8vo

'ART III.—A SELECTION OF WORKS OF FICTION

nnett (Arnold)—
CLAYHANGER, 8s. *net.* HILDA LESSWAYS, 8s. 6d. *net.* THESE TWAIN. THE CARD. THE REGENT: A Five Towns Story of Adventure in London. THE PRICE OF LOVE. BURIED ALIVE. A MAN FROM THE NORTH. THE MATADOR OF THE FIVE TOWNS. WHOM GOD HATH JOINED. A GREAT MAN: A Frolic. *All 7s. 6d. net.*

rmingham (George A.)—
SPANISH GOLD. THE SEARCH PARTY. LALAGE'S LOVERS. THE BAD TIMES. UP, THE REBELS. *All 7s. 6d. net.* INISHEENY, 8s. 6d. *net.* THE LOST LAWYER, 7s. 6d. *net.*

urroughs (Edgar Rice)—
TARZAN OF THE APES, 6s. *net.* THE RETURN OF TARZAN, 6s. *net.* THE BEASTS OF TARZAN, 6s. *net.* THE SON OF TARZAN, 6s. *net.* JUNGLE TALES OF TARZAN, 6s. *net.* TARZAN AND THE JEWELS OF OPAR, 6s. *net.* TARZAN THE UNTAMED, 7s. 6d. *net.* A PRINCESS OF MARS, 6s. *net.* THE GODS OF MARS, 6s. *net.* THE WARLORD OF MARS, 6s. *net.* THUVIA, MAID OF MARS, 6s. *net.* TARZAN THE TERRIBLE, 2s. 6d. *net.* THE MAN WITHOUT A SOUL. 6s. *net.*

nrad (Joseph). A SET OF SIX, 7s. 6d. *net.* VICTORY: An Island Tale. *Cr. 8vo.* 9s. *net.* THE SECRET AGENT: A Simple Tale. *Cr. 8vo.* 9s. *net.* UNDER WESTERN EYES. *Cr. 8vo.* 9s *net.* CHANCE. *Cr. 8vo.* 9s *net.*

Corelli (Marie)—
A ROMANCE OF TWO WORLDS, 7s. 6d. *net.* VENDETTA: or, The Story of One Forgotten, 8s. *net.* THELMA: A Norwegian Princess, 8s. 6d. *net.* ARDATH: The Story of a Dead Self, 7s. 6d. *net.* THE SOUL OF LILITH, 7s. 6d. *net.* WORMWOOD: A Drama of Paris, 8s. *net.* BARABBAS: A Dream of the World's Tragedy, 8s. *net.* THE SORROWS OF SATAN, 7s. 6d. *net.* THE MASTER-CHRISTIAN, 8s. 6d. *net.* TEMPORAL POWER: A Study in Supremacy, 6s. *net.* GOD'S GOOD MAN: A Simple Love Story, 8s. 6d. *net.* HOLY ORDERS: The Tragedy of a Quiet Life, 8s. 6d. *net.* THE MIGHTY ATOM, 7s. 6d. *net.* BOY: A Sketch, 7s. 6d. *net.* CAMEOS, 6s. *net.* THE LIFE EVERLASTING, 8s. 6d. *net.* THE LOVE OF LONG AGO, AND OTHER STORIES, 8s. 6d. *net.* INNOCENT, 7s. 6d. *net.* THE SECRET POWER: A Romance of the Time, 7s. 6d. *net.*

Hichens (Robert)—
TONGUES OF CONSCIENCE, 7s. 6d. *net.* FELIX: Three Years in a Life, 7s. 6d. *net.* THE WOMAN WITH THE FAN, 7s. 6d. *net.* BYEWAYS, 7s. 6d. *net.* THE GARDEN OF ALLAH, 8s. 6d. *net.* THE CALL OF THE BLOOD, 8s. 6d. *net.* BARBARY SHEEP, 6s. *net.* THE DWELLER ON THE THRESHOLD, 7s. 6d. *net.* THE WAY OF AMBITION, 7s. 6d. *net.* IN THE WILDERNESS, 7s. 6d. *net.*

Hope (Anthony)—
A CHANGE OF AIR. A MAN OF MARK. THE CHRONICLES OF COUNT ANTONIO. SIMON DALE. THE KING'S MIRROR. QUISANTÉ. THE DOLLY DIALOGUES. TALES OF TWO PEOPLE. A SERVANT OF THE PUBLIC. MRS. MAXON PROTESTS. A YOUNG MAN'S YEAR. BEAUMAROY HOME FROM THE WARS. *All 7s. 6d. net.*

Jacobs (W. W.)—
MANY CARGOES, 5s. *net.* SEA URCHINS, 5s. *net* and 3s. 6d. *net.* A MASTER OF CRAFT, 5s. *net.* LIGHT FREIGHTS, 5s. *net.* THE SKIPPER'S WOOING, 5s. *net.* AT SUN-WICH PORT, 5s. *net.* DIALSTONE LANE, 5s. *net.* ODD CRAFT, 5s. *net.* THE LADY OF THE BARGE, 5s. *net.* SALTHAVEN, 5s. *net.* SAILORS' KNOTS, 5s. *net.* SHORT CRUISES, 6s. *net.*

London (Jack). WHITE FANG. *Ninth Edition. Cr. 8vo. 7s. 6d. net.*

Lucas (E. V.)—
LISTENER'S LURE : An Oblique Narration, 6s. *net.* OVER BEMERTON'S: An Easy-going Chronicle, 6s. *net.* MR. INGLESIDE, 6s. *net.* LONDON LAVENDER, 6s. *net.* LANDMARKS, 7s. 6d. net. THE VERMILION BOX, 7s. 6d *net.* VERENA IN THE MIDST, 8s. 6d. *net.* ROSE AND ROSE, 7s. 6d. *net.*

McKenna (Stephen)—
SONIA : Between Two Worlds, 8s. *net.* NINETY-SIX HOURS' LEAVE, 7s. 6d. *net.* THE SIXTH SENSE, 6s. *net.* MIDAS & SON, 8s. *net.*

Malet (Lucas)—
THE HISTORY OF SIR RICHARD CALMADY : A Romance. 10s. *net.* THE CARISSIMA. THE GATELESS BARRIER. DEADHAM HARD. *All 7s. 6d. net.* THE WAGES OF SIN. 8s. *net.*

Mason (A. E. W.). CLEMENTINA. Illustrated. *Ninth Edition. Cr. 8vo. 7s. 6d. net.*

Maxwell (W. B.)—
VIVIEN. THE GUARDED FLAME. ODD LENGTHS. HILL RISE. THE REST CURE. *All 7s. 6d. net.*

Oxenham (John)—
PROFIT AND LOSS. THE SONG OF HYACINTH, and Other Stories. THE COIL OF CARNE. THE QUEST OF THE GOLDEN ROSE. MARY ALL-ALONE. BROKEN SHACKLES. "1914." *All 7s. 6d. net.*

Parker (Gilbert)—
PIERRE AND HIS PEOPLE. MRS. FALCHIO. THE TRANSLATION OF A SAVAGE. WHE VALMOND CAME TO PONTIAC : The Story a Lost Napoleon. AN ADVENTURER OF TI NORTH : The Last Adventures of 'Pret Pierre.' THE SEATS OF THE MIGHTY. TI BATTLE OF THE STRONG: A Roman of Two Kingdoms. THE POMP OF TI LAVILETTES. NORTHERN LIGHTS. *A 7s. 6d. net.*

Phillpotts (Eden)—
CHILDREN OF THE MIST. THE RIVE DEMETER'S DAUGHTER. THE HUMAN B(AND THE WAR. *All 7s. 6d. net.*

Ridge (W. Pett)—
A SON OF THE STATE, 7s. 6d. net. TI REMINGTON SENTENCE, 7s. 6d. *ne* MADAME PRINCE, 7s. 6d. *net.* TOP SPEE 7s. 6d. *net.* SPECIAL PERFORMANCES, 6 *net.* THE BUSTLING HOURS, 7s. 6d. *ne* BANNERTONS AGENCY, 7s. 6d. *net.* WEL TO-DO ARTHUR, 7s. 6d. *net.*

Rohmer (Sax)—
THE DEVIL DOCTOR. TALES OF SECRE EGYPT. THE ORCHARD OF TEARS. TI GOLDEN SCORPION. *All 7s. 6d. net.*

Swinnerton (F.). SHOPS AND HOUSE *Third Edition. Cr. 8vo. 7s. 6d. net.*
SEPTEMBER. *Third Edition. Cr. 8* 7s. 6d. net.
THE HAPPY FAMILY. *Second Editio* 7s. 6d. net.
ON THE STAIRCASE. *Third Editio* 7s. 6d. net.
COQUETTE. *Cr. 8vo. 7s. 6d. net.*

Wells (H. G.). BEALBY. *Fourth Editio Cr. 8vo. 7s. 6d. net.*

Williamson (C. N. and A. M.)—
THE LIGHTNING CONDUCTOR: The Stran Adventures of a Motor Car. LADY BETT ACROSS THE WATER. LORD LOVELAN DISCOVERS AMERICA. THE GUESTS (HERCULES. IT HAPPENED IN EGYPT. SOLDIER OF THE LEGION. THE SH(GIRL. THE LIGHTNING CONDUCTRES SECRET HISTORY. THE LOVE PIRAT *All 7s. 6d. net.* CRUCIFIX CORNER. 6 *net.*

Methuen's Two-Shilling Novels

Cheap Editions of many of the most Popular Novels of the day

Write for Complete List

Fcap. 8vo

CPSIA information can be obtained
at www.ICGtesting.com
Printed in the USA
LVHW080503110321
681206LV00004B/16